OPPOSING
VIEWPOINTS®
SERIES

DNA Testing
and Privacy

Other Books of Related Interest

Opposing Viewpoints Series

Big Pharma and Drug Pricing
Hacking and Freedom of Information
Scientific Research

At Issue Series

Biological and Chemical Weapons
DNA Databases
Extending the Human Lifespan

Current Controversies Series

Genetic Engineering
Medical Ethics
Privacy and Security in the Digital Age

"Congress shall make no law … abridging the freedom of speech, or of the press."

First Amendment to the US Constitution

The basic foundation of our democracy is the First Amendment guarantee of freedom of expression. The Opposing Viewpoints series is dedicated to the concept of this basic freedom and the idea that it is more important to practice it than to enshrine it.

OPPOSING
VIEWPOINTS®
SERIES

DNA Testing and Privacy

Barbara Krasner, Book Editor

GREENHAVEN
PUBLISHING

Published in 2020 by Greenhaven Publishing, LLC
353 3rd Avenue, Suite 255, New York, NY 10010

First Edition

Articles in Greenhaven Publishing anthologies are often edited for length to meet page
requirements. In addition, original titles of these works are changed to clearly present
the main thesis and to explicitly indicate the author's opinion. Every effort is made to
ensure that Greenhaven Publishing accurately reflects the original intent of the authors.
Every effort has been made to trace the owners of the copyrighted material.

Cover image: Bill O'Leary/The Washington Post via Getty Images

Library of Congress Cataloging-in-Publication Data

Names: Krasner, Barbara, editor.
Title: DNA testing and privacy / Barbara Krasner, book editor [compiling
  editor].
Other titles: Opposing viewpoints series (Unnumbered)
Description: First edition. | New York : Greenhaven Publishing, 2020. |
  Series: Opposing viewpoints | Audience: Grades 9 to 12. | Includes
  bibliographical references and index.
Identifiers: LCCN 2019003292 | ISBN 9781534505001 (library bound) | ISBN
  9781534505018 (pbk.)
Subjects: LCSH: DNA—Analysis—Juvenile literature. | DNA
  fingerprinting—Juvenile literature. | DNA data banks—Juvenile
  literature. | Privacy, Right of—Juvenile literature.
Classification: LCC QP624 .D17497 2020 | DDC 614/.1—dc23
LC record available at https://lccn.loc.gov/2019003292

Manufactured in the United States of America

Website: http://greenhavenpublishing.com

Contents

Chapter 3: Should DNA Testing Reveal the Consumer's Identity?

Chapter 4: Should Testing Companies Share Genetic Data with Research Partners?

The Importance of Opposing Viewpoints

Perhaps every generation experiences a period in time in which the populace seems especially polarized, starkly divided on the important issues of the day and gravitating toward the far ends of the political spectrum and away from a consensus-facilitating middle ground. The world in which today's students are growing up and into which they will soon enter as active and engaged citizens is deeply fragmented in just this way. Issues relating to terrorism, immigration, women's rights, minority rights, race relations, health care, taxation, wealth and poverty, the environment, policing, military intervention, the proper role of government—in some ways, perennial issues that are freshly and uniquely urgent and vital with each new generation—are currently roiling the world.

If we are to foster a knowledgeable, responsible, active, and engaged citizenry among today's youth, we must provide them with the intellectual, interpretive, and critical-thinking tools and experience necessary to make sense of the world around them and of the all-important debates and arguments that inform it. After all, the outcome of these debates will in large measure determine the future course, prospects, and outcomes of the world and its peoples, particularly its youth. If they are to become successful members of society and productive and informed citizens, students need to learn how to evaluate the strengths and weaknesses of someone else's arguments, how to sift fact from opinion and fallacy, and how to test the relative merits and validity of their own opinions against the known facts and the best possible available information. The landmark series Opposing Viewpoints has been providing students with just such critical-thinking skills and exposure to the debates surrounding society's most urgent contemporary issues for many years, and it continues to serve this essential role with undiminished commitment, care, and rigor.

The key to the series's success in achieving its goal of sharpening students' critical-thinking and analytic skills resides in its title—

Opposing Viewpoints. In every intriguing, compelling, and engaging volume of this series, readers are presented with the widest possible spectrum of distinct viewpoints, expert opinions, and informed argumentation and commentary, supplied by some of today's leading academics, thinkers, analysts, politicians, policy makers, economists, activists, change agents, and advocates. Every opinion and argument anthologized here is presented objectively and accorded respect. There is no editorializing in any introductory text or in the arrangement and order of the pieces. No piece is included as a "straw man," an easy ideological target for cheap point-scoring. As wide and inclusive a range of viewpoints as possible is offered, with no privileging of one particular political ideology or cultural perspective over another. It is left to each individual reader to evaluate the relative merits of each argument— as he or she sees it, and with the use of ever-growing critical-thinking skills—and grapple with his or her own assumptions, beliefs, and perspectives to determine how convincing or successful any given argument is and how the reader's own stance on the issue may be modified or altered in response to it.

This process is facilitated and supported by volume, chapter, and selection introductions that provide readers with the essential context they need to begin engaging with the spotlighted issues, with the debates surrounding them, and with their own perhaps shifting or nascent opinions on them. In addition, guided reading and discussion questions encourage readers to determine the authors' point of view and purpose, interrogate and analyze the various arguments and their rhetoric and structure, evaluate the arguments' strengths and weaknesses, test their claims against available facts and evidence, judge the validity of the reasoning, and bring into clearer, sharper focus the reader's own beliefs and conclusions and how they may differ from or align with those in the collection or those of their classmates.

Research has shown that reading comprehension skills improve dramatically when students are provided with compelling, intriguing, and relevant "discussable" texts. The subject matter of these collections could not be more compelling, intriguing, or urgently relevant to today's students and the world they are poised to inherit. The anthologized articles and the reading and discussion questions that are included with them also provide the basis for stimulating, lively, and passionate classroom debates. Students who are compelled to anticipate objections to their own argument and identify the flaws in those of an opponent read more carefully, think more critically, and steep themselves in relevant context, facts, and information more thoroughly. In short, using discussable text of the kind provided by every single volume in the Opposing Viewpoints series encourages close reading, facilitates reading comprehension, fosters research, strengthens critical thinking, and greatly enlivens and energizes classroom discussion and participation. The entire learning process is deepened, extended, and strengthened.

For all of these reasons, Opposing Viewpoints continues to be exactly the right resource at exactly the right time—when we most need to provide readers with the critical-thinking tools and skills that will not only serve them well in school but also in their careers and their daily lives as decision-making family members, community members, and citizens. This series encourages respectful engagement with and analysis of opposing viewpoints and fosters a resulting increase in the strength and rigor of one's own opinions and stances. As such, it helps make readers "future ready," and that readiness will pay rich dividends for the readers themselves, for the citizenry, for our society, and for the world at large.

Introduction

> *"This isn't a videogame, it's people's*
> *genetic code and it's a very*
> *valuable commodity."*

> *—Peter Pitts, president,*
> *Center for Medicine in*
> *the Public Interest[1]*

Over Thanksgiving weekend in 2017, AncestryDNA sold 1.5 million DNA testing kits.[2] Packed neatly inside the kits come terms of service agreements. Most likely, those are swiftly tossed aside in the zeal for ancestral or health information. A simple cheek swab or spit in a vial can reveal genetic secrets held in a person's DNA. But other secrets may lurk within those service agreements. They include: Who owns the person's DNA data? Do testing companies reserve the rights to it? Can they sell the data without the person knowing? Is a person's identity revealed when these sales happen?

In general, most people don't read the fine print in service agreements. In taking an at-home DNA test, this has particular repercussions, because these agreements contain terms about privacy and data sharing. Not reading the fine print before agreeing to the terms means people may be relieving themselves unknowingly of certain important rights to their own genetic information. For instance, testing companies, such as 23andMe, AncestryDNA, MyHeritageDNA, and FamilyTreeDNA, insist that no data can be shared without the consumers' permission. They may even insist that people have the option to delete their individual test results from testing company databases at any time. Yet these testing companies may also argue that they require perpetual, royalty-free transferable license of DNA data. They contend this license would allow them to perform a variety of functions: hosting, transfer, analysis, distribution, and communication of genetic information. An agreement may promise use of DNA test results to advance medical research for Parkinson's disease, and contributing to the research may be important to the test-taker. However, promises may not be fulfilled. Further, the data license may just be used to promote the testing companies' products and services (as well as from other organizations) for years to come. Some pundits argue that this is where testing companies make their revenue and profit; they do not make their money from selling testing kits directly to consumers.

But taking at-home DNA tests may provide some advantages, too. Consumers can choose how they want their anonymized DNA sample shared with others. Data could be used for a specific type of analysis that interests them such as diabetes research. This act of goodwill ultimately could help to resolve important health issues. Consumers can also choose to connect or not to connect to other people as a result of their analyses. This is done through a consumer-supplied username.

The very nature of DNA raises others concerns about identifiability. Health experts and legal advocates may warn users about the possibility of connecting their identities to DNA code. That said, little of the data is actually used. A person's genome has about three billion units of DNA. Two-thirds of that is shared with other people. DNA tests only examine somewhere between five and seven percent of the unique remaining code. Plus, DNA data on one individual could take up thousands of pages of code. Some experts maintain it is not possible to identify a single individual, so there's no privacy risk involved in sharing the data. Yet, others contend that DNA code is still ultimately unique to an individual. Even without name identification, it can only be associated with one person.

That connection may become vulnerable to attacks. When sending in a saliva sample to a DNA testing company, a consumer becomes known by an identification number. Only when the results are produced are the identification number and consumer name connected. Yet, hackers have been able to infiltrate databases and with the help of other database information, including credit card data, infringe upon privacy. However, criminal investigators have successfully used genealogy databases to crack cases open. For example, investigators identified the Golden State Killer, a man responsible for at least twelve murders and fifty rapes between 1974 and 1986, by using a genealogy website's open-source database. They were unable to gain access to the databases of Ancestry and 23andMe.

While DNA may be useful in finding such criminals, it may also prove helpful in finding long-lost relatives, birth parents, and other family connections. In the public television show *Finding Your Roots*, host scholar Henry Louis Gates Jr. routinely used DNA testing to help his guests find family. However, testing may also cause irreparable damage to existing family relationships. A person may find he or she is not the biological child of one or both parents. These discoveries may rip apart existing family relationships with little hope of reconciliation, leaving the person with the DNA results wondering whether the test was worth it.

With news about DNA testing companies making frequent headlines, policy makers are calling for regulation, including federal laws to protect consumers' rights. In Germany, for example, only physicians can order genetic tests. It can be argued that these rights should be considered as civil rights. One federal law, the Genetic Information Non-Discrimination Act, prohibits employers from using genetic data against potential employees in the hiring process. Federal lawmakers are now insisting that testing companies clarify their security and privacy policies. The Federal Trade Commission issued a warning in 2017 to be wary of who else might profit from consumers' DNA results.

Opposing Viewpoints: DNA Testing and Privacy explores the complex issues surrounding the widespread use of commercial testing to discover our genetic code and how the results are used.

In chapters titled "Who Owns DNA Test Results?" "Should Testing Companies Reserve Some Rights to DNA Data?" "Should DNA Testing Reveal the Consumer's Identity?" and "Should Testing Companies Share Genetic Data with Research Partners?" viewpoints tackle challenging questions that address health, legal, family, and ethical issues debated by leading scholars, health care professionals, researchers, policy makers, and journalists.

Notes

1. Megan Molten, "Ancestry's Genetic Testing Kits Are Heading for Your Stocking This Year," Wired, December 1, 2017, accessed October 1, 2018, https://www.wired.com/story/ancestrys-genetic-testing-kits-are-heading-for-your-stocking-this-year/.

2. Ibid.

OPPOSING
VIEWPOINTS®
SERIES

CHAPTER 1

Who Owns DNA Test Results?

Chapter Preface

A DNA testing kit arrives in a person's mailbox. Inside the kit are instructions that include online registration. The person, in his zeal to unlock the secrets of his ancestry or medical predispositions, eagerly keys in the website address and clicks through the terms of agreement, not bothering to read any of the fine print.

This experience is typical of a DNA test-taker. But that service agreement carefully outlines privacy and ownership rights of the person's DNA information. While the agreements of the leading DNA test companies—Ancestry, 23andMe, My Heritage, and FamilyTree—claim consumers own the rights to their own data, they also reserve rights to license the data, that is, to collect, store, analyze, and distribute results. The question arises: Who owns DNA test results?

Genetic information is the most intimate and unique information a person has. No one else can own that DNA. However, others can own DNA analysis or claim they do. Service agreements promise consumers can opt out of sharing their data with third parties and that they can remove their data from the company's database. A simple click in the service agreement's Informed Consent section allows companies to do what they want with consumer genetic data. Few people pay much attention to this, and according to some experts, freely give away their rights to the most sensitive information they own.

There are other privacy concerns as well. Testing company databases could be hacked. Data analysis may be inaccurate, as each testing company may provide a different result based on the size, scope, and composition of its own database. Database results could backfire. They could identify a consumer and/or a genetic relative as a carrier of a particular disease. Health insurance companies could potentially use this data to refuse coverage.

The following chapter investigates DNA testing company policies and terms of service to determine the rights of the consumer and the rights of the testing company. The authors of the viewpoints express opposing perspectives about who actually controls and owns DNA data gained through at-home testing kits.

> *"You have complete control over how the DNA companies use your DNA. You can choose to be paired to potential relatives or not. You can opt into or out of research programs that could lead to medical breakthroughs. And you can delete your results whenever you like."*

Testing Companies Claim Consumers Own Their Genetic Information

Leah Larkin

In the following viewpoint, Leah Larkin argues that while lawmakers are calling attention to the potentially harmful use of people's DNA data in the hands of third parties, there are many positives to bear in mind. Key among these advantages is that the consumer has control over whether his or her sensitive genetic code information is shared with others, including possible relatives, and with third-party companies. At the core of the argument lie the consent terms in testing company service agreements. Leah Larkin is cofounder and lead genealogist at the DNA Geek. She holds a PhD in biology from the University of Texas at Austin.

"Who Owns Your Genetic Information?" The DNA Geek, December 3, 2017. Reprinted by permission.

As you read, consider the following questions:

1. What evidence does the author provide to show no prohibitions in at-home DNA testing?
2. What evidence is provided in the viewpoint here to counter that position?
3. What does "informed consent" mean to the DNA testing companies?

Senator Chuck Schumer recently kicked the undercurrent of paranoia about DNA testing up a notch in a press conference filled with inaccurate information. He said, "Here's what many consumers don't realize, that their sensitive information can end up in the hands of unknown third-party companies. There are no prohibitions, and many companies say that they can still sell your information to other companies."

"There are no prohibitions." That's simply not true. Worse, Schumer's press conference sparked some grossly irresponsible clickbait "journalism" stoking fears of DNA testing.

Not All Journalism Is Good Journalism

Let's unpack some of this using this article in Gizmodo [https://gizmodo.com/sen-chuck-schumer-wants-the-ftc-to-take-a-serious-look-1820769045] as an example. It contains inflammatory statements like "you're giving up unfettered access to information about what makes you, you." This statement is wrong on a number of levels. First, you're not giving up "unfettered access" to anything. You have complete control over how the DNA companies use your DNA. You can choose to be paired to potential relatives or not. You can opt into or out of research programs that could lead to medical breakthroughs. And you can delete your results whenever you like.

On a biological level, the statement is ridiculous for two reasons. First, your genome contains roughly 3 billion units of DNA, and most of it is identical to other humans. Only about 10 million of those units are SNPs (pronounced "snips" and short for single nucleotide polymorphisms), meaning they vary among people. The DNA tests we do for genealogy only look at about 500,000 to 700,000 SNPs. So, of the 10 million units of DNA that differentiate me from the rest of humanity, the tests look at only 5% to 7%.

Second, fewer than 10% of the SNPs the genealogy testing companies use are known or suspected to have any effect on us. The vast majority of our DNA has no function at all. That's right: most of those SNPs don't contribute a thing to "what makes you, you." For example, SNPedia, a wiki for genetic information, listed only 107,582 SNPs as of 3 December 2017. Their criterion for listing a SNP in the wiki is "something worthy of recording." In other words, the other 9,892,418 SNPs in the human genome don't do anything that we know of. AncestryDNA looks at fewer than half of the SNPedia SNPs, and the other companies examine even fewer. (Thanks to Dr. Ann Turner for pointing me to the SNPedia page that lists how many genetically meaningful SNPs are tested by each genealogy company.)

But there's more. The Gizmodo author writes "the breadth of rights you are giving away to your DNA when you spit in that vial is kind of crazy. It's all there in the fine print: Testing companies can claim ownership of your DNA, allow third parties to access it, and make your DNA vulnerable to hackers." Ai-yi-yi! First, the "fine print" states that you own your own genetic information, with one possible exception; more on that below. And the companies do not allow third parties to access it without your permission. True, anything online is vulnerable to hackers, but what the heck would a hacker do with a fraction of your genome, most of which has no function?

One last beef with the Gizmodo article before I move on. It says, "23andMe, for example, sell anonymized data from your genetic code to its research partners, to help put all that genetic data to use looking for cures to diseases. That's a use most people probably wouldn't mind. But that research partner could in turn share your anonymized data in a research journal, and it's possible someone might identify it." The author of this piece has obviously never tried to identify someone using DNA alone. If it were so easy, the DNA Detectives Facebook group wouldn't have more than 72,000 members, each of whom spends weeks or months or years trying to identify a single biological parent. The author has also clearly never read a research journal. Your raw data file from one of the testing companies contains literally hundreds of thousands of rows of text. Just for fun, I opened one of mine in Microsoft Word; the program stopped counting pages when it got to 10,000. The type of research study that could lead to medical breakthroughs would involve thousands of participants. It takes a special kinda … something … to think a journal would actually publish millions of pages of raw data, even if ethical guidelines allowed it, which they don't.

Selling Your Genetic Information

Let's cut to the chase: Can the companies sell your DNA information to third parties? Yes, they can. All of them include wording in their policies allowing them to share or sell our genetic information, but only if you agree to let them do it. What's in the fine print?

AncestryDNA Terms and Conditions: "Any sharing of Genetic Information for external research purposes is governed by the Informed Consent."

23andMe Privacy Policy: "We will not sell, lease, or rent your individual-level information (i.e., information about a single individual's genotypes, diseases or other traits/characteristics) to any third-party or to a third-party for research purposes without your explicit consent."

MyHeritage Privacy Policy: "We will never sell or license DNA samples, DNA Results, DNA Reports or any other DNA information, to any third parties without your explicit informed consent."

Family Tree DNA Privacy Policy: "Gene by Gene respects your privacy and will not sell or rent your Personal Information without your consent. Personal Information includes, but is not limited to names, phone numbers, physical or mailing addresses, email addresses, and genetic test results." (Gene by Gene is the parent company of Family Tree DNA.)

In summary, all four companies have the exact same policy with respect to sharing or selling our data to third parties: they do it only if we give them permission. The permission is granted to a company when you opt into their research program.

Who "Owns" Your Genetic Information?

Again, I'll let the companies speak for themselves. Note that the "rights" granted in their agreements are what they need to provide the ethnicity estimates and relative matching that we pay them for.

AncestryDNA Terms and Conditions: "AncestryDNA does not claim any ownership rights in the DNA that is submitted for testing. Any Genetic Information (your DNA data and any information derived from it) belongs to the person who provided the DNA sample, subject only to the rights granted to AncestryDNA in this Agreement."

23andMe Terms of Service: "Any Genetic Information derived from your saliva remains your information, subject to rights we retain as set forth in these TOS."

MyHeritage Terms and Conditions: "We do not claim any ownership rights in the DNA samples, the DNA Results and/or the genetic information in the DNA Reports. Any genetic information derived from the DNA samples, the DNA Results and/or appears in the DNA Reports [sic] continues to belong to the person from whom the DNA was collected, subject only to the rights granted to MyHeritage in this Agreement."

Family Tree DNA Privacy Policy and Terms of Service: "While the DNA sample remains the property of the tester, the person paying retains rights to the test results. If the tester decides to have results removed from the website, the tester must refund the full purchase price to the purchaser(s) and provide documentation to Family Tree DNA of the transaction." Elsewhere, they say, "The owner of an account is responsible for naming a beneficiary to that account, should the test taker pass away. If no beneficiary is named on the account, Family Tree DNA retains ownership of the record and DNA. If a family member or heir presents documentation of relationship to the deceased test taker, Family Tree DNA may, at its discretion, allow the family member or heir access to the account."

Wait, what?

To be honest, I'm not sure what to think here. In a recent press release, Bennett Greenspan, the Founder and CEO of Family Tree DNA (FTDNA), said "We feel the only person that should have your DNA is you. We don't believe it should be sold, traded, or bartered." Yet, we've already seen that their policy with respect to selling data is the same as the other companies. What's more, FTDNA is the only company reviewed in this post that never explicitly states in their Terms of Service that we own our genetic information. (They allude to the fact that we own the samples—the cheek swabs—but not the genetic data itself.) And if someone else gave us the test, that other person has equal rights to our results until we pay them back.

Their beneficiary policy is also worrisome. A will is a legally binding declaration of what happens to our possessions when we die. If I own my genetic information, I should be able to bequeath it in my will to whomever I like. But FTDNA is saying that, unless I designate a beneficiary in their system, my will only applies at their discretion. The use of the phrase "retains ownership" is another big red flag. They can't "retain ownership" of something that's mine. That wording implies that we don't own our genetic information at FTDNA; they do.

To summarize, at AncestryDNA, 23andMe, and MyHeritage, the person who takes the test owns the genetic information in it. At FTDNA, at best ownership is unclear and at worst, it belongs to FTDNA. I would like to see FTDNA revise their Terms of Service and Privacy Policy to explicitly state that we own our genetic information, regardless of who paid for the test, and that ownership does not revert to FTDNA when we die.

Informed Consent

What happens to our genetic information if we consent to participate in a research study at one of the companies?

AncestryDNA Informed Consent: "Consenting to participate in this research is completely voluntary and is not required to use any of our products or services. Even if you consent to participate in the research, you may withdraw your consent at any time, but your information will not be removed from research that is in progress or completed."

23andMe Research Consent Document: "Your participation in the 23andMe Research study is completely voluntary." And, "you can withdraw from 23andMe Research at any time. Any of your data that have already been entered into a study cannot be withdrawn, but your data will not be included in studies that start more than 30 days after you withdraw (it may take up to 30 days to withdraw your information after you withdraw your consent)."

MyHeritage Informed Consent Agreement: "Participation in this Project is purely voluntary and may be revoked at any time. If you choose to withdraw some or all of your personally identifiable information you provided to the Project, you may do so by contacting us to advise of your withdrawal. Upon your withdrawal, we will cease using your DNA Results in the Project. We will continue to provide you with the ability to use the Website or the DNA Services as before. Please note that due to the de-identification of certain Research Information, any research or studies using anonymized or aggregate information that has already begun, studies that have been completed, and any study results or findings that have been published prior to your withdrawal cannot be reversed, undone, or removed."

Family Tree DNA Privacy Policy, Additional Consent: "Additionally, your consent will be sought for research purposes. Much of the genetic information resulting from DNA testing has not been clinically validated, and the technology we use, which is the same technology used by the research community, to date has not been widely used for clinical testing. For these reasons, our customers are encouraged to participate in Gene by Gene's research initiatives that may contribute to a better understanding of the results of genetic testing. Your participation in these initiatives is entirely voluntary and your DNA test results will not be used or disclosed without your consent. Once given, however, consent cannot be revoked." [original emphasis]

Per the US Department of Health and Human Services: "Subjects have the right to withdraw from (i.e., discontinue participation in) research at anytime (45 CFR 46.116(a)(8))." FTDNA needs to change their wording regarding the withdrawal of consent.

The big picture? You have complete control over whether to participate in the research programs, and you can withdraw your consent at any time. The one thing you can't do is pull your data from a research study that's already been published or that is underway.

Schumer

I don't blame Schumer. He's trying to do what politicians are supposed to do, which is to respond to the concerns of his constituents. He's undoubtedly heard from enough residents of New York state, which he represents, to spur him to action. The problem is that he's misguided about the "dangers" of DNA testing with the major genealogical companies, and, as a result, is proposing a government solution to something that isn't a problem. And in doing so, he's stoking irrational fear that will scare people away from a fun and rewarding hobby.

"Basically, Ancestry.com gets to use or distribute your DNA for any research or commercial purpose it decides and doesn't have to pay you, or your heirs, a dime."

Buyer Beware! AncestryDNA Can Identify You and Your Genetic Relatives

Joel Winston

In the following viewpoint, Joel Winston argues that consumers should not use AncestryDNA's testing service without knowing what they are agreeing to in the terms of service. He maintains that test-takers own DNA, but so does Ancestry. He insists that every consumer should read DNA test service agreements. Joel Winston is a nationally recognized advocate for consumer protection and privacy law. He has appeared on C-SPAN, CNN, and many other venues as an expert. He earned his JD degree from Seton Hall University in New Jersey and operates a law practice in New York City.

"Ancestry.com Takes DNA Ownership Rights From Customers and Their Relatives," by Joel Winston, ThinkProgress, May 17, 2017. Reprinted by permission.

As you read, consider the following questions:

1. What are the three significant provisions in the AncestryDNA Privacy Policy and Terms of Service people should know?
2. How can a testing company have identifiable parts of your DNA if a person has never taken a test?
3. What does the author identify as a "massive red flag"?

Don't use the AncestryDNA testing service without actually reading the Ancestry.com Terms of Service and Privacy Policy. According to these legal contracts, you still own your DNA, but so does Ancestry.com.

The family history website Ancestry.com is selling a new DNA testing service called AncestryDNA. But the DNA and genetic data that Ancestry.com collects may be used against "you or a genetic relative." According to its privacy policies, Ancestry.com takes ownership of your DNA forever. Your ownership of your DNA, on the other hand, is limited in years.

It seems obvious that customers agree to this arrangement, since all of them must "click here to agree" to these terms. But, how many people really read those contacts before clicking to agree? And how many relatives of Ancestry.com customers are also reading?

There are three significant provisions in the AncestryDNA Privacy Policy and Terms of Service to consider on behalf of yourself and your genetic relatives: (1) the perpetual, royalty-free, world-wide license to use your DNA; (2) the warning that DNA information may be used against "you or a genetic relative"; (3) your waiver of legal rights.

1. Perpetual, Royalty-Free, Worldwide License to Use Your DNA

AncestryDNA, a service of Ancestry.com, owns the "World's Largest Consumer DNA Database" that contains the DNA of more than 3 million people. The AncestryDNA service promises to, "uncover your ethnic mix, discover distant relatives, and find new details about your unique family history with a simple DNA test."

For the price of $99 dollars and a small saliva sample, AncestryDNA customers get an analysis of their genetic ethnicity and a list of potential relatives identified by genetic matching. Ancestry.com, on the other hand, gets free ownership of your genetic information forever. Technically, Ancestry.com will own your DNA even after you're dead.

Specifically, by submitting DNA to AncestryDNA, you agree to "grant AncestryDNA and the Ancestry Group Companies a perpetual, royalty-free, world-wide, transferable license to use your DNA, and any DNA you submit for any person from whom you obtained legal authorization as described in this Agreement, and to use, host, sublicense and distribute the resulting analysis to the extent and in the form or context we deem appropriate on or through any media or medium and with any technology or devices now known or hereafter developed or discovered."

Basically, Ancestry.com gets to use or distribute your DNA for any research or commercial purpose it decides and doesn't have to pay you, or your heirs, a dime. Furthermore, Ancestry.com takes this royalty-free license in perpetuity (for all time) and can distribute the results of your DNA tests anywhere in the world and with any technology that exists, or will ever be invented. With this single contractual provision, customers are granting Ancestry.com the broadest possible rights to own and exploit their genetic information.

The AncestryDNA terms also requires customers to confirm that, "You understand that by providing any DNA to us, you acquire no rights in any research or commercial products that may be developed by AncestryDNA that may relate to or otherwise embody your DNA." Essentially, you still own your DNA, but so does Ancestry.com. And, you can commercialize your own DNA for money, but Ancestry.com is also allowed to monetize your DNA for millions of dollars and doesn't have to compensate you.

Although AncestryDNA customers provide voluntary consent to have their DNA used in commercial research projects, customers are free to withdraw consent, with a few exceptions. First, "data cannot be withdrawn from research already in progress or completed, or from published results and findings." In those cases, Ancestry.com has access to data about you indefinitely.

Secondly, if a customer withdraws their consent, Ancestry.com will take 30 days to cease using their data for research. Finally, withdrawing consent, "will not result in destruction of your DNA Sample or deletion of your Data from AncestryDNA products and services, unless you direct us otherwise." Customers must jump through additional hoops if they want their DNA sample destroyed or their data deleted from AncestryDNA products and services. The Ancestry.com policy does not specify what "additional steps" are required. US customers must contact Ancestry.com customer service at 1–800–958–9124 to find out. (Customers outside the United States must call separate customer service numbers.)

2. Warning That DNA Information May Be Used Against "You or a Genetic Relative"

The Ancestry.com DNA testing service promises to analyze approximately 700,000 genetic markers. According to Ancestry.com, the service, "combines advanced DNA science with the world's largest online family history resource to predict your genetic ethnicity and help you find new family connections." The results of an AncestryDNA analysis include information about "ethnicity across 26 regions/ethnicities and identifies potential relatives through DNA matching to others who have taken the AncestryDNA test."

AncestryDNA claims to use the "latest autosomal testing technology" to produce genetic identity reports and can combine the test results with "the world's largest online family history resource to predict your genetic ethnicity and help you find new family connections." In addition, AncestryDNA offers a genetic code profiling and matching service, advertising that

"AncestryDNA can also help identify relationships with unknown relatives through a dynamic list of DNA matches."

This raises a thorny issue that Ancestry.com has not resolved: your exact DNA profile is unique to you, but a substantial portion of your DNA is identical to your relatives. Thus, Ancestry.com is able to take DNA from its customers and also their relatives. Even if you've never used Ancestry.com, but one of your genetic relatives has, the company may already own identifiable portions of your DNA.

The personal "Genetic Data" collected by Ancestry.com includes "information derived from processing your DNA Sample through genomic, molecular, and computational analyses using various technologies, such as genotyping and whole or partial genome sequencing. Genetic Data is broader than just the results delivered to you when you use the AncestryDNA test and includes a range of DNA markers such as those associated with your health or other conditions." In short, Ancestry.com holds genetic data that reveals your health and other conditions.

Genetic diseases are disorders caused by abnormalities in a person's DNA and are divided into three categories: single-gene disorders, such as cystic fibrosis, sickle cell disease, and Huntington's disease, result from the mutation of the protein of a single gene; chromosome abnormalities, such as Down Syndrome, are caused by disorders of the whole chromosome; and multifactorial disorders, including breast cancer and Alzheimer's disease, develop from mutations in multiple genes, often coupled with environmental causes. Genomics play a role in nine out of the top ten leading causes of death in the US, including cancer, heart disease, stroke, chronic lower respiratory diseases, diabetes, Alzheimer's, influenza and pneumonia, septicemia, and kidney disease.

Buried in the "Informed Consent" section, which is incorporated into the Terms of Service, Ancestry.com warns customers, "it is possible that information about you or a genetic relative could be revealed, such as that you or a relative are carriers of a particular disease. That information could be used by insurers to deny you insurance coverage, by law enforcement agencies to identify you or your relatives, and in some places, the data could be used by employers to deny employment."

This is a massive red flag. The data "you or a genetic relative" give to AncestryDNA could be used against "you or a genetic relative" by employers, insurers, and law enforcement.

For example, a young woman named Theresa Morelli applied for individual disability insurance, consented to release of her medical records through the Medical Information Bureau (a credit reporting agency for medical history), and was approved for coverage. One month later, Morelli's coverage was cancelled and premiums refunded when the insurer learned her father had Huntington's disease, a genetic illness.

Startlingly, the Medical Information Bureau (MIB) used Morelli's broad consent to query her father's physician, a doctor with whom she had no prior patient relationship. More importantly, the applicant herself wasn't diagnosed with Huntington's carrier status, but she suffered exclusion on the basis of a genetic predisposition in her family.

Under a 1995 consent agreement with the Federal Trade Commission, the MIB and its members are required to comply with consumer protections of the Fair Credit Reporting Act. Much like financial credit reports, all consumers are entitled to a free annual copy of their "medical report" file from the Medical Information Bureau (MIB). If the consumer discovers an error in her MIB medical credit report file, she must mail a letter to the MIB to begin the dispute process.

Federal laws, including the Health Insurance Portability and Accountability Act of 1996 (HIPAA) and the Genetic Information Non-Discrimination Act of 2008 (GINA), contain protections that prohibit health insurers from requiring, using, and analyzing genetic information in health care coverage decisions. However, both laws contain glaring exceptions that allow for genetic discrimination in certain industries. Notably, no federal laws regulate the use of genetic information, genetic testing, and genetic discrimination for life insurance companies, long-term care insurers, and employers.

An Ancestry.com DNA test is the impetus of a federal civil rights lawsuit filed by Sergeant Cleon Brown, a white police officer in Hastings, Michigan against his employer, the Hastings Police Department, and several city employees. Curious about his own family history, Brown purchased an AncestryDNA genetic test and analysis report.

The results surprised him—Ancestry.com said his DNA was 18 percent sub-Saharan African. Brown "proudly told his colleagues at the police department" about his African ancestry.

But not long after that, "his elation turned into misery." According to Sergeant Brown's complaint, his colleagues at the police department, "started whispering 'Black Lives Matter' while pumping their fists as they walked" past Brown.

The complaint also alleges that the former mayor of Hastings participated in the racist teasing, by telling Brown a joke containing racist slurs. "I just never thought it would be in Hastings, saying, like, racist comments to me," Brown said to the *New York Times*. In his lawsuit, Brown, a military veteran who has worked in law enforcement for 20 years, is seeking $500,000 in damages.

The Ancestry.com Terms of Service also warns that genetic information in its possession can be used by state or federal law enforcement agencies "to identify you or your relatives." With the rise of forensic evidence in criminal investigations, DNA is often considered incontrovertible evidence. To propel the use of DNA evidence in criminal investigations and prosecutions, the Federal Bureau of Investigation (FBI) operates the national Combined DNA Index System (CODIS) database.

The CODIS DNA database, created and maintained by the FBI, consists of the following three levels of information: local DNA Index Systems (LDIS) where DNA profiles originate; state DNA Index Systems (SDIS) which allows for laboratories within states to share information; and the National DNA Index System (NDIS) which allows states to compare DNA information with one another. According to reports, the FBI's CODIS software connects disparate databases including, arrestees, missing persons, convicted offenders, and forensic samples collected from crime scenes.

All 50 states, the District of Columbia, federal law enforcement, the Army Laboratory, and Puerto Rico participate in national sharing of DNA profiles through the CODIS system. However, the FBI DNA database is not infallible. In 2015, the FBI said it discovered flawed data after it commissioned a study to retest DNA samples. In a bulletin sent to crime labs across the United States, the FBI surmised that DNA data errors were probably due to "clerical mistakes in transcriptions of the genotypes and to limitations of the old technology and software." The FBI suspects that errors in DNA may go back as far as 1999.

3. Waiver of Legal Rights

Are "you or a genetic relative" a customer of AncestryDNA? If so, Ancestry.com now has control over the DNA of "you or a genetic relative." Should the warnings from Ancestry.com come to pass, and DNA information about "you or a genetic relative" is used against "you or a genetic relative" by any employer, insurer, or law enforcement, then "you or a genetic relative" have very limited legal rights.

In its sales contract, Ancestry.com takes no responsibility. By consenting to the AncestryDNA Terms and Conditions, "you or a genetic relative" agree to hold the company harmless for any damages that AncestryDNA may cause unintentionally or purposefully. If "you or a genetic relative" are "dissatisfied with any portion of the Websites or the Services, or with any clause of these terms, as your sole and exclusive remedy you may discontinue using the Websites and the Services." The only option for unhappy customers is to stop using AncestryDNA.

In the event you or your genetic information cause harm, you agree to "defend, indemnify and hold harmless AncestryDNA, its affiliates, officers, directors, employees and agents from and against any and all claims, damages, obligations, losses, liabilities, costs or expenses (including but not limited to attorney's fees)." And customers beware, "you may be liable to others as well as to us if your account is used in violation of the terms and conditions of this Agreement." That means you could end up owing money to Ancestry.com, its attorneys, and others.

The final indignity for Ancestry.com customers is that they must waive fundamental legal rights by agreeing to mandatory binding arbitration. With the exception of intellectual property rights disputes and certain small claims, Ancestry.com customers must pursue their disputes through arbitration, rather than court. In arbitration, the established legal rules of discovery, evidence, and trial by jury do not exist.

Finally, if many AncestryDNA customers want to join together to file a lawsuit against Ancestry.com, they are prohibited. But in fairness, Ancestry.com similarly prohibits itself from joining with a bunch of others to file a class action lawsuit against you. By agreeing to the Terms and Conditions, "you and AncestryDNA agree that each may bring claims against the other only in your or its individual capacity, and not as a plaintiff or class member in any purported class, consolidated, or representative action."

These arbitration provisions survive even if you cancel your AncestryDNA account. However, for good measure, Ancestry. com notes that, "this arbitration agreement does not preclude you from bringing issues to the attention of federal, state, or local agencies. Such agencies can, if the law allows, seek relief against us on your behalf."

4. Conclusion

To use the AncestryDNA service, customers must consent to the Ancestry.com Privacy Policy and Terms of Service. These are binding legal contracts between the customer and Ancestry.com. The most egregious of these terms gives Ancestry.com a free license to exploit your DNA for the rest of time.

Customers must understand that turning over their DNA means a loss of complete ownership and control. Ancestry.com customers should also know they're giving up the genetic privacy of themselves and their relatives.

Before purchasing, individuals are advised to fully read and consider the Ancestry.com Terms of Service and Privacy Policy. If you become a customer, Ancestry.com owns your DNA for life and longer.

Editor's Note: After the publication of this piece, Ancestry. com released a statement and made some changes to its Terms and Conditions. The organization has not responded to multiple requests for clarification from the author of this piece, and there are still remaining concerns about customers' privacy.

"In the future, if genetic data becomes commonplace enough, people might be able to pay a fee and get access to someone's genetic data, too, the way we can now to access someone's criminal background."

A DNA Data Breach Could Mean Rejections of Insurance, Credit, and Employment—or Worse

Angela Chen

In the following viewpoint, Angela Chen argues that a recent breach of MyHeritage's database of consumer DNA data signals a trend to come in the near future. Genetic data will attract hackers for potential lucrative sale to third parties. She suggests that genetic data held by testing companies need to adhere to legal protections akin to the Health Insurance Portability and Accountability Act (HIPAA). Angela Chen is a science reporter for The Verge. *She previously worked as a staff reporter at the* Wall Street Journal. *Her writing has appeared in* The Guardian, The Atlantic, Chronicle of Higher Education, Smithsonian, *and other leading magazines.*

"Why A DNA Data Breach Is Much Worse than A Credit Card Leak," by Angela Chen, Vox Media, Inc., June 6, 2018. Reprinted by permission.

As you read, consider the following questions:

1. Why would hackers want DNA data? What could they do with it?
2. What are some of the types of companies that could benefit from people's DNA information?
3. In what way could the DNA information be wrong?

This week, DNA testing service MyHeritage revealed that hackers had breached 92 million of its accounts. Though the hackers only accessed encrypted emails and passwords—so they never reached the actual genetic data—there's no question that this type of hack will happen more frequently as consumer genetic testing becomes more and more popular. So why would hackers want DNA information specifically? And what are the implications of a big DNA breach?

One simple reason is that hackers might want to sell DNA data back for ransom, says Giovanni Vigna, a professor of computer science at UC Santa Barbara and co-founder of cybersecurity company Lastline. Hackers could threaten to revoke access or post the sensitive information online if not given money; one Indiana hospital paid $55,000 to hackers for this very reason. But there are reasons genetic data specifically could be lucrative. "This data could be sold on the down-low or monetized to insurance companies," Vigna adds. "You can imagine the consequences: One day, I might apply for a long-term loan and get rejected because deep in the corporate system, there is data that I am very likely to get Alzheimer's and die before I would repay the loan."

MyHeritage doesn't offer health or medical tests, but many companies, like 23andMe and Helix, do. And there are plenty of players interested in DNA: researchers want genetic data for scientific studies, insurance companies want genetic data to help them calculate the cost of health and life insurance, and police want genetic data to help them track down criminals, like in the recent Golden State Killer case. Already, we lack robust protections

DNA Strands Used to Hack Computer

Researchers from the University of Washington say they have successfully hacked into a computer using custom strands of DNA for the first time.

Akin to something from the pages of science fiction, the researchers used the life-encoding molecule to attack and take over a computer, using strands of DNA to transmit a computer virus from the biological to the digital realm.

"We designed and created a synthetic DNA strand that contained malicious computer code encoded in the bases of the DNA strand," wrote the researchers led by Tadayoshi Kohno and Luis Ceze from the Paul G Allen school of computer science and engineering at the University of Washington.

The hack was only possible because of weakness in the DNA sequencing software, and only in this specific instance. The researchers say that there is no reason for concern: "Note that there is not present cause for alarm about present-day threats. We have no evidence to believe that the security of DNA sequencing or DNA data in general is currently under attack."

"Hacking a Computer Using DNA Is Now A Reality, Researchers Claim," by Samuel Gibbs, Guardian News and Media Limited, August 11, 2017.

when it comes to genetic privacy, and so a genetic data breach could be a nightmare. "If there is data that exists, there is a way for it to be exploited," says Natalie Ram, a professor of law focusing on bioethics issues at the University of Baltimore.

Genetic testing sites are treasure troves of sensitive information. Some sites offer users the option to download a copy of their full genetic code while others don't. But the full genetic code isn't the most valuable information anyway. As Ram points out, we can't just read genetic code like a book to gain insights. Instead, it's the easy-to-access account pages with health interpretations that are most useful for hackers.

This is the data that could be valuable to insurance companies, employees, and police. In a world where this data is posted online, it could be used to genetically discriminate against people, such as denying mortgages or increasing insurance costs. (It doesn't help that interpreting genetics is complicated and many people don't understand the probabilities anyway.) In the future, if genetic data becomes commonplace enough, people might be able to pay a fee and get access to someone's genetic data, too, the way we can now to access someone's criminal background.

Of course, police and companies would not want to actively work with hackers. But it can be unclear where the data comes from, and there will always be underground markets through which this information could be bought and sold, or used as blackmail. "I can't imagine that, once this information is hacked and put on the web, it would have more protection than before," says Ram. "I don't think we can say that simply because some data was the result of a hack, no one is ever going to touch it. That would be unrealistic."

Another problem complicates this issue: These consumer tests are often wrong. Health reports can offer up false positives, and even ancestry tests can be wildly inaccurate. For example, some 23andMe tests have been approved by the FDA, but others haven't, meaning there are other results that could be inaccurate.

So while it's possible for someone to receive a credit report and easily dispute it, almost no one has the genetic literacy to find their information, understand it, and correct it. There aren't enough genetic counselors as it is and a recent study showed that some primary care providers didn't feel comfortable interpreting the results.

As the Equifax hack last year showed, there's a lack of legislation governing what happens to data from a breach. And ultimately, a breach of genetic data is much more serious than most credit breaches. Genetic information is immutable: Vigna points out that it's possible to change credit card numbers or even addresses, but genetic information cannot be changed. And genetic information is often shared involuntarily. "Even if I don't use 23andMe, I have cousins who did, so effectively I may be genetically searchable," says Ram. In one case, an identical twin having her genetic data sequenced created a tricky situation for her sister.

Ram thinks we need to consider whether genetic-testing companies have a greater ethical obligation to their customers, and seriously consider how to prevent and deal with breaches. For example, privacy protections for medical data exist and are covered under the Health Insurance Portability and Accountability Act. For now, results from consumer genetic testing aren't covered under HIPAA, but one option could be to change the law so that these results are included, too. "We put a lot of trust in these consumer companies that are promising to help us understand who we are genetically" says Ram. But there a lot of questions about how much they can teach us and there's a lot of big questions about what kinds of caveats they really ought to make sure their users understand what they're looking at, and how they can be protected."

> "With the three companies we spoke with, none of them will share your genetic data with others for research purposes unless you explicitly opt in, and even then, that data will be de-identified."

Testing Companies Do Not Share Your Data Without Your Consent

Rob Verger

In the following viewpoint, Rob Verger argues that consumers must opt in to an agreement with a testing company to share their genetic information. Through an analysis of 23andMe, AncestryDNA, and Living DNA, he concludes that test-taker data are safe and anonymized. For all three companies, customers can ultimately request their accounts and DNA samples be expunged. Rob Verger is a science and technology journalist, currently serving as Assistant Tech Editor at Popular Science. *He has written for* Newsweek, The Daily Beast, The Boston Globe, *the* Columbia Journalism Review, *and other publications.*

"Here's What Kind of Data Genetics Testing Companies Can Share," by Rob Verger, *Popular Science*, May 30, 2018. Reprinted by permission.

As you read, consider the following questions:

1. Does the presentation of three company cases make for compelling evidence?
2. Is dealing with a company that also offers newspapers a riskier choice for consumers? Why or why not?
3. What is "individual data sharing consent" offered by 23andMe?

It's natural to want to scratch at the itch of identity—and these days you can, for about $99. Mail a little tube full of spit, or a cheek swab, to a laboratory, and they'll tell you about who you are on a genetic level. Companies like Living DNA, AncestryDNA, and 23andMe offer this service: a chance to learn more about your ethnicity and ancestry.

But in a time of the Facebook and Cambridge Analytica scandal, other data breaches, and the GDPR, it's also natural to wonder: What happens when I share my genetic information—a biological sample—with companies?

Here's the short answer: With the three companies we spoke with, none of them will share your genetic data with others for research purposes unless you explicitly opt in, and even then, that data will be de-identified—meaning any outside organization that sees it, in any form, won't know it came from you. And in all cases, if you are an existing customer, you can contact the company and ask them to delete your account, your genetic data, and even throw out the sample you mailed them.

Curious to know more about each company—what they share with others, and how to delete your data? Here's a breakdown.

Living DNA

Living DNA, a company based in Frome, England, offers a genetics testing service that they advertise as highly detailed while at the same time putting an emphasis on privacy. Of the three companies we spoke with, it is the only one that does not share research data with at least one separate, for-profit company.

"We do not sell your data," says David Nicholson, Living DNA's cofounder. "We do not work with pharmaceutical companies."

Customers can choose to opt into a research project run by the company, though, and if they do, their data could be included in it. In that case, the information would be de-identified and aggregated with other information from other people. That investigation is focused on "mapping of the world DNA" and involves "working with academic institutions," Nicholson says. Any customer who opts into that research can subsequently choose to remove themselves from future study later, but data that the company has already folded into the research cannot be extracted. Anyone who wants to know more about this study can read more here.

Living DNA is a for-profit company (like the others in this story), so their page describing their research does contain this disclaimer: "This may result in patents and other intellectual property for Living DNA."

Like other companies, Living DNA says that they will erase all the data they have, including the physical sample you sent them. "You have full rights to destroy all info that we hold upon you, including all your genetic data," Nicholson says. The only exceptions to this are the internal financial records Living DNA has—they can't just delete the fact that someone paid them for a test.

Nicholson also notes that while the laboratory they work with only sees DNA samples with a barcode on them, and not customers' names or other information, the lab does keep the records they need to for regulatory reasons. "For some parts of the lab process, there is an aggregative bit of information that's needed as part of our regulatory approval," he says. "We have to actually prove that each sample has been run accurately."

If you are a customer of Living DNA, and you want them to delete everything they have on you that they are capable of erasing, email privacy@livingdna.com or help@livingdna.com. Nicholson says that in the future customers will be able to do this through their account settings.

AncestryDNA

In its privacy policy, Ancestry says they value transparency, simplicity, and control. Anyone who has had their ethnicity tested through them (and it's a service that I personally have tried) can have their account and genetic data deleted, and their physical DNA sample as well.

Like Living DNA, Ancestry conducts research with the genetic information it has, but only for customers who have explicitly opted into participating in it. The information they share with their collaborators is de-identified. Of the organizations they work with, one is a separate, for-profit company: Calico Life Sciences LLC, which according to a statement, focuses "on longevity research and therapeutics."

Customers can opt-out of the research if they've previously opted in, but any information that's already been shared with their partners can't be unshared. (And as always, that genetic info is anonymized.)

Ancestry also owns other brands, like newspapers.com, so someone who signs up for Ancestry DNA could receive emails advertising those products. Finally, an Ancestry spokesperson says that in the past, they have worked with other vendors to market products to customers. That means that an Ancestry user could receive an email from the company with an offer for a product that involves a third-party company, but the spokesperson says they don't currently make those types of offers now. If you wanted something like your family tree on a mug, they worked with a third-party to make that happen.

In short, the Ancestry spokesperson says that they don't sell data (like a customer list) for marketing purposes, but they do use third parties to help them do their own marketing, like hawking their newspaper.com-type services.

ANCESTRYDNA STILL CLAIMS TO OWN YOUR DNA

AncestryDNA, owned by the company behind family-tree website Ancestry.com, has taken at least one step toward making its policies more transparent. The company's privacy policy and terms of use agreements have been updated so that they are actually easy to understand for anyone with a basic command of English.

If you want to make an informed decision about how your biological data is going to be used, being able to understand the policies that dictate data use is key.

"This is a good step," Joel Winston, a consumer protection lawyer, told Gizmodo. "All this information is readable, and it's all in one place."

That said, the digestibility of the privacy policies that govern companies like AncestryDNA and 23andMe is only one part of the problem. Ancestry didn't actually change any of its policies themselves. In its new language, for example, Ancestry is emphatic that you retain ownership over your DNA, repeating in many places statements like this one:

"You own your DNA data and you can ask us to remove your data from our systems at any time."

"Ancestry Made Its Privacy Policy More Transparent, But It Still Claims to Own Your DNA," by Kristen V. Brown, Gizmodo Media Group, January 11, 2018.

If you are an Ancestry customer and want your data deleted, and your DNA sample thrown out, you can do so by navigating to this address.

23andMe

Each person has 23 pairs of chromosomes in their cells, a fact that gives 23andMe its name. When someone signs up for a genetic test through the company, they can choose whether to have them hold onto their sample if, in the future, 23andMe has more services to offer and thus can re-test the sample. Someone who chooses to have their sample bio-banked can later change their mind and have it discarded.

Like with the other companies, customers can opt into research or not. The privacy officer for 23andMe, Kate Black, says that about 80 percent of their customers do opt-in, and that when they do, their de-identified data is shared with their partners in an aggregated way. "For example," Black says, "if one of our partners was interested in understanding more about Parkinson's, we would be able to tell them that about 30 percent of the individuals in our database have a specific gene associated with Parkinson's."

In addition, 23andMe customers can choose to have their data shared on a more specific level—an option called the "individual data sharing consent." That would include genetic information about a specific person, but the person would not be identified by name nor would the researchers see any contact information for them.

Someone who opts into being a part of research for 23andMe, on either level, and later opts out, can't have what's already shared with outsiders removed (the same is true with the other two companies). But Black says that if someone does say they no longer want to be a part of the research, the company will stop sharing their data with their partners 30 days from when that request is made.

If you want to know more about the organizations that 23andMe shares data with, this page lists some of them, which include the University of Chicago, and the Lupus Research Institute. Some of the organizations they work with are for-profit, like Pfizer, but 23andMe does not publicly name all of them. "We don't make a full list available, but the information on the website is completely representative," Black says.

In short: if you sign up for 23andMe and don't like the idea of your data—in any form—being shared with companies like Biogen or Pfizer, simply do not consent to that option. It's not required.

Anyone who wants to delete the information that 23andMe has can do so through the "23andMe Data" section in their account settings, and can read their full privacy policy here.

Periodical and Internet Sources Bibliography

The following articles have been selected to supplement the diverse views presented in this chapter.

Seth Axelrad, "State Statutes Declaring Genetic Information to be Personal Property," *American Society of Law, Medicine, and Ethics*, n.d. www.aslme.org/dna_04/reports/axelrad4.pdf.

Marcus Baram, "The FTC Is Investigating DNA Firms like 23andMe and Ancestry Over Privacy," *Fast Company*, June 5, 2018. www.fastcompany.com/40580364/the-ftc-is-investigating-dna-firms-like-23andme-and-ancestry-over-privacy.

James Bell, "You Own Your DNA, But Ancestry DNA Claim They Still Own It Too," *Frontline Genomics*, January 12, 2018. www.frontlinegenomics.com/news/18260/ancestry-dna-update-policies-own-your-dna/.

Jacob Brogan, "Who Owns Your Genetic Data After a Home DNA Test," *Slate*, May 23, 2017. https://slate.com/technology/2017/05/ancestrydnas-terms-and-conditions-sparked-a-debate-about-ownership-of-genetic-material.html.

Kristen V. Brown, "What DNA Testing Companies' Terrifying Privacy Policies Actually Mean," Gizmodo, October 19, 2017. https://gizmodo.com/what-dna-testing-companies-terrifying-privacy-policies-1819158337.

Kashmala Fida, "DNA Ancestry Testing Poses Privacy Risks, Alberta Health Expert Warns," Toronto Star Newspapers Limited, May 8, 2018. https://www.thestar.com/edmonton/2018/05/07/ancestry-dna-testing-poses-privacy-risks-health-expert-warns.html.

Erika Fry and Sy Mukherjee, "Do DNA Testing Companies Like 23andMe Own Your Biological Data?" *Fortune*, March 19, 2018. fortune.com/2018/03/19/dna-testing-23andme-owns-biological-data/.

Erica Gunderson, "What DNA Testing Kits Can – and Can't – Tell You About History, Health," WTTW, January 11, 2018. https://news.wttw.com/2018/01/11/what-dna-testing-kits-can-and-can-t-tell-you-about-history-health.

Eric Heath, "Setting the Record Straight: Ancestry and Your DNA," Ancestry DNA, May 21, 2017. https://blogs.ancestry.com/ancestry/2017/05/21/setting-the-record-straight-ancestry-and-your-dna/.

Carolyn Johnston, Jane Kay, Jessica Bell, Megan Prictor, and Harriet Teare, "Who Owns Your DNA?" Pursuit/University of Melbourne, November 26, 2017. pursuit.unimelb.edu.au/articles/who-owns-your-dna.

Michele Loi, "Nobody's DNA But Mine." *Journal of Medical Ethics* 44, no. 11 (November 2018).

Thomas MacEntee, "How Secure Are Your DNA Test Results? What You Should Know About Privacy BEFORE You Take a DNA Test!" *Abundant Genealogy*, April 23, 2018. abundantgenealogy.com/dna-testing-balancing-value-and-privacy/.

Dan MacGuill, "Can Ancestry.com Take Ownership of Your DNA Data?" Snopes.com, May 23, 2017. www.snopes.com/fact-check/ancestry-dna-steal-own/.

Eric Rosenbaum, "5 Biggest Risks of Sharing Your DNA with Consumer Genetic-Testing Companies," CNBC, June 16, 2018. www.cnbc.com/2018/06/16/5-biggest-risks-of-sharing-dna-with-consumer-genetic-testing-companies.html.

Molly Wood, "Who Owns the Results of Genetic Testing?" *Marketplace*, October 16, 2018. www.marketplace.org/2018/10/16/tech/who-owns-results-genetic-testing.

OPPOSING
VIEWPOINTS®
SERIES

CHAPTER 2

Should Testing Companies Reserve Some Rights to DNA Data?

Chapter Preface

DNA testing company service agreements may state they require rights to consumer samples for analysis. Experts argue that companies offering direct-to-consumer DNA testing kits make their money by selling additional products and services and by selling the DNA data to third parties. If one of these testing companies is sold, it cannot guarantee continued privacy of the data. Further privacy breaches occur when genetic data with no associated consumer name is combined with other database information to identify the person.

Several companies have made DNA data the center of their products and services. They claim that DNA analysis helps to customize choices such as meal planning, wine selection, skin care, and even finding the most suitable roommate. Once these companies have people's DNA data, they can compile it and sell it. DNA data mining has become a hot market.

No regulation has full jurisdiction over this market, either, making it a free-for-all for companies to dupe consumers. Legal experts, government officials, and consumer advocates call for legislation to protect consumer genetic information privacy without going to the extreme of stipulating that only physicians can order DNA testing. They wonder whether the Health Insurance Portability and Accountability Act (HIPAA) could be applied to genetic data farmed by companies like 23andMe and MyHeritageDNA. They also wonder whether the Genetic Information Nondiscrimination Act (GINA) goes far enough to protect consumer privacy.

Yet, despite all the misgivings about violating consumer privacy, there are cases where DNA data can be put to good use. 23andMe, for instance, offered DNA tests to refugees so they could locate family members. Certain rights of the companies must be upheld to make these connections happen. This company, along with AncestryDNA and MyHeritageDNA, issued new privacy guidelines in 2018 to respond to public criticism of their privacy practices.

The following chapter considers whether DNA testing companies should have certain rights to the genetic data they collect and analyze. The authors of the viewpoints present opposing opinions about the use of this data and its alleged protections beyond the consumers' initial intent.

"Almost 50 percent of the firms that sell you your ancestry information turn around and sell your genetic information to some other company."

When Testing Companies Retain Rights They Can Sell Consumer Data

Genevieve Rajewski

In the following viewpoint, Genevieve Rajewski interviews Sheldon Krimsky, a Tufts University professor and board chair of the Council for Responsible Genetics. The interview reveals privacy issues that consumers, such as adoptees, must understand before agreeing to the testing company's terms of service. Even when the data is de-identified, it can still be associated with a specific individual. The interview also addresses accuracy issues and insists users be prepared for surprise. Genevieve Rajewski is Senior Writer and Editor for Tufts University's Cummings Veterinary Medicine Magazine *in Wakefield, Massachusetts.*

As you read, consider the following questions:

1. In what ways can a DNA test be inaccurate?
2. According to this viewpoint, can a person's DNA information be shared without consent? If so, how? If not, what are the protections?
3. How do testing companies use their own reference databases?

For my family this past holiday season, the most heated discussion was not generated from the usual suspects (politics or sibling dynamics), but rather from a Secret Santa gift: a 23andMe genetics testing kit given by an aunt to her niece. The kit's premise is that by sending in a saliva sample, you can find out how much of your DNA hails from different parts of the world.

The niece was thrilled. She said that, being half African American, she longed to know what region of Africa her ancestors had come from. But she and other family members voiced concerns about whether her genetic information and material would be sold to the highest bidder, to be used for research—or worse.

No one in the family understood all the ins and outs of ancestry DNA tests like 23andMe, so I took our questions to Sheldon Krimsky, the Lenore Stern Professor of Humanities and Social Sciences and an adjunct professor in public health and community medicine at Tufts. Krimsky, author of Genetic Justice and board chair of the Council for Responsible Genetics, recently co-wrote "Ancestry DNA Testing and Privacy: A Consumer Guide."

For consumers, the most important thing is to "make sure you're prepared for surprise, whether it's a correct or incorrect one," he said. "Are you an odd mixture? Probably; most of us are. Ancestry tests are trying to give people a simple answer to what chances are was a much more complex past."

Tufts Now: How accurate are these tests when it comes to determining ethnicity and genealogy?

Sheldon Krimsky: We don't really know, because the companies selling these services—and there are close to 40 of them—don't share their data, and their methods are not validated by an independent group of scientists and there are not agreed-upon standards of accuracy. People have sent their DNA to several of these companies and found differences in the results—though not necessarily radical differences. So you have to look at the percentages you receive back with skepticism.

Why do the tests return different results?

Each company offering these services uses its own proprietary database of DNA samples called ancestry informative markers (AIMs) from current populations in Asia, Africa, Europe, and the Americas. From within those databases, they each select for a certain number of alleles—one member of a pair of genes located at a specific position on a specific chromosome—and in these spots, use the genetic variations known as single nucleotide polymorphisms (SNPs) as the basis for evaluating individuals. The markers—SNPs—are chosen because they have different frequencies across different geographical populations.

They compare SNPs with those most frequently associated with different populations in their reference database. The results are in no way definitive; instead each company uses common genetic variations as the basis for saying the probability is that 50 percent of your DNA is, for example, from North Europe and 30 percent is from Asia, based on how it compares to the information in its database. However, if you send DNA to a second company, you might get different results, because it has a different database. Studies that have compared ancestry databases have found poorer concordance with Hispanic, East Asian, and South Asian descent.

What else might make your ancestry results inaccurate?

There's a big chunk of data—actually the majority—that these genetics-testing services don't use. Your DNA contains millions of SNPs, but these tests are selectively looking at certain genetic variations and use between 100 to 300 AIMs, which account for a small part of the SNPs that differentiate the human family. So even if a test says you are 50 percent European, really it can only report that half of those SNPs of your DNA looks to be European.

The results are further skewed by the fact that certain ancestry information markers used by any particular test may come from only your paternal line (Y chromosome) or your maternal line (mitochondrial DNA). Tests using these markers are less accurate.

Finally, these testing services use DNA from modern populations in these regions to draw conclusions about people who lived in those areas hundreds or thousands of years ago. It's a big leap to assume that the particular SNPs used by the tests have remained constant for all that time.

Does my family member have any hope of finding out where the African-American side of her family came from?

It's possible to learn something about her past, if she's lucky. She can perhaps find out what percentage of her genetic markers match favorably with markers seen in different regions of Africa, but only if the AIMs can distinguish different regions. West African AIMs are the most frequently used for inferring African ancestry. And if she were to do ancestry tests with two or three different companies, she might have a pretty good idea if her markers show a high or moderate similarity to those of people currently living in different parts of Africa, if those companies have the appropriate reference populations.

She has to understand that she's not matching her DNA to someone from hundreds of years ago. It's also quite possible for someone who is African American to get ancestry test results

Two Federal Agencies Regulate Genetic Tests

Two federal agencies have the primary authority to regulate genetic tests: the Food and Drug Administration (FDA) and the Centers for Medicare and Medicaid Services (CMS). In the past, the Federal Trade Commission (FTC) has also played a role in regulating genetic testing companies who advertised false and misleading claims about their products, but this agency currently plays a more minor role in this space.

Genetic and Genomic tests, like other types of diagnostic tests, can be evaluated and regulated on the following three criteria:*

- **Analytical Validity:** Refers to how well the test predicts the presence or absence of a particular gene or genetic change. Can the test consistently and accurately detect whether a specific genetic variant is present or absent?
- **Clinical Validity:** Refers to how well the genetic variant(s) being analyzed is related to the presence, absence, or risk of a specific disease. Has having a specific genetic variant been conclusively shown to increase the risk or likelihood of having a disease or eventually developing a disease?
- **Clinical Utility:** Refers to whether the test can provide information about diagnosis, treatment, management, or prevention of a disease that will be helpful to patients and their providers. Will use of the test lead to improved health outcomes?

* Definitions are adapted from the National Library of Medicine's Genetics Home Reference.

"Regulation of Genetic Tests," U.S. Department of Health and Human Services, January 17, 2018.

that say they're 75 percent European. That's because the chosen ancestry-information markers reflect only a small percentage of our DNA, and there's actually more genetic diversity within the African population than between the African population and a European population. (For more about this, see dialogue one in a publication I co-wrote, "Using Dialogues to Explore Genetics, Ancestry, and Race.")

What are the privacy issues with these tests?

The companies offering these tests largely make their money not from doing the tests, but from selling the genetic information to other companies interested in having access to large genetic databases. Almost 50 percent of the firms that sell you your ancestry information turn around and sell your genetic information to some other company.

Often these are pharmaceutical companies trying to understand how variations in certain sections of the human genome may be useful in drug development. (Certain drugs may not function as well in a person carrying certain mutations, so the companies want to find the frequency of these mutations in the population.) Only about 10 percent of the companies that offer ancestry tests destroy your original sample; the vast majority hold onto your sample or sell it. So it's not just the data, but your actual saliva, that's being shopped around.

The companies offering testing services often go up for sale, and their privacy policies typically indicate that they bear no responsibility for your privacy once the company is sold—anything you signed is not reliable anymore. Many of the companies have privacy policies that state they can be changed at any time without notifying previous signers. In effect, you need to keep in contact with the company and keep yourself up-to-date on its policy. How many people are going to do that?

There's also a lot of concern that even though your name is not listed on the database, when the data is sold to somebody, the records can be de-anonymized. It has happened before—people have been able to take genetic information with no name on it and, through other databases, find the name associated with that genetic material.

A co-worker told me that his sister, who was adopted, learned she had a half-sibling after doing one of these tests, and was really excited to find a new family member. But if I learned I had a half-sibling somewhere, that news would be something of a bombshell.

Yes, some of the companies selling these testing services give you the option of learning about people who have similar SNPs to you. You can get a list of people who may appear to be part of your larger family ancestry, and with permission you can contact them or they can contact you. On the surface this sounds innocuous and entertaining, but it certainly can raise questions that people might not be ready for.

For example, there are people who don't know exactly where they came from. You may have thought your grandmother was your mother, because you were raised as sister to your actual mother.

Not everyone wants to hear that kind of information. I don't know that people who sign up with these services fully understand all the possible implications of the results they could receive back.

> "*Beyond the quick buck, though, many of the companies are also playing a long game. Once they sell customers' data, they can compile it and sell it to researchers. ...That's where there's real money to be made.*"

There's a Buck to Be Made by Testing DNA for Reasons Other Than Ancestry

Emily Mullin

In the following viewpoint, Emily Mullin argues that DNA testing companies—beyond those testing for ancestry—are mainly looking to make their money and profit by selling customers additional products and services. She cites Lean Cuisine's Nutria, skincare company SkinGenie, wine curator Vinome, and roommate app SpareRoom. Emily Mullin is a Baltimore, Maryland–based science journalist focused on medicine, health, and biotechnology. She is a former associate editor for biomedicine at MIT Technology Review. Her work has also been published in Scientific American, The Atlantic, National Geographic, Smithsonian, The Washington Post, *and other publications.*

"These DNA Testing Companies Are Mainly Trying to Sell You Other Stuff," by Emily Mullin, MIT Technology Review, April 26, 2018. Reprinted by permission.

As you read, consider the following questions:

1. Can the companies cited in this viewpoint make a real connection using DNA?
2. What is the purpose of the questionnaires these companies administer?
3. According to this viewpoint, what do experts say about the ability of DNA to make personal product recommendations?

The consumer genetics market is booming. In 2017, the number of people who took direct-to-consumer ancestry tests more than doubled, reaching over 12 million customers.

The at-home DNA testing craze is quickly expanding outside of ancestry, too. A wave of new tests claims to make all sorts of personalized lifestyle recommendations—from skincare products to diet—based on your genes. But experts say that while genetics certainly underpins many of our characteristics, there's little scientific evidence that the genetic element of these tests makes the interventions they recommend especially effective.

Many of these tests contain a survey or questionnaire about your habits, health and other personal information. While the tests often do provide some insights about your DNA, their product recommendations might come mostly from analyzing your answers to the survey and common-sense advice. "When someone who is selling you a test says you need this product, you should question their motives," says James Evans, a physician and geneticist at the University of North Carolina School of Medicine.

Here are some tests you might want to think twice about before sending away a DNA sample.

Nutria

The pitch: Lean Cuisine, the well-known purveyor of frozen meals, is trying out a new meal-planning service that involves a DNA test. It claims that its "genetic markers help determine your customized nutrient intake," but the service also includes a survey that asks about your food preferences, allergies, and lifestyle.

The price: At $79 for eight weeks (it's in a trial phase), the program offers recommendations for recipes, dining-out options, and prepared meals (probably from Lean Cuisine).

The science: It also includes an app that allows you to connect with a nutritionist. That's probably more useful than the DNA analysis: a recent study published in the *Journal of the American Medical Association* found that diets based on DNA results didn't help people lose weight. Other companies, like Nutrigene and LifeDNA, want to sell you vitamin supplements on the basis of a DNA test.

SkinGenie

The pitch: SkinGenie says it will give you personalized recommendations of skincare products based on a lifestyle quiz and a DNA analysis. The company says this can be done without the DNA analysis, but it can give you a "more accurate assessment" with a DNA sample.

The price: The skincare assessment costs $59, and that's after purchasing a DNA test kit through LifeNome or uploading your raw data from 23andMe, Ancestry.com, or another company. If you just want to view the product ranking without the skin assessment, you can upload your DNA data at no cost.

The science: SkinGenie's report looks at 120 genetic markers associated with more than 30 different skin characteristics. It uses this genetic readout to give you a personal ranking (out of 10) of skincare products based on their active ingredients. SkinGenie says these recommendations are based on thousands of research studies. But Evans says our "limited knowledge about how genes are involved in the integrity of our skin can't be used to design tailored products or care"—at least not yet. Plus, factors other

TESTING COMPANY ACCESS TO DNA DATA COULD MEAN FOREVER

You might be intrigued by what your genes could tell you about your ancestry or the health risks hidden in your DNA. If so, you're not alone.

Fascination with personal genetics is fuelling an explosion of online DNA testing. More than 12 million people have been tested—7 million through ancestry.com alone. Amazon reported the 23andMe online DNA test kit as one of its top five best-selling items on Black Friday in 2017.

But while online genetic testing can be interesting and fun, it has risks.

Some online genetic testing companies don't comply with international guidelines on privacy, confidentiality and use of genetic data. Many online testing companies retain DNA samples indefinitely. Consumers can request samples be destroyed, but sometimes have difficulties with this.

Some online testing companies have been accused of selling access to databases of genetic information to third parties, potentially without the knowledge of donors. You might have to plough through the fine print to find out what you have consented to.

In many ways, it is wonderful we now have access to our personal DNA code. However, as always, understanding the limitations and risks of fast-moving medical technology is very important.

"Five Things to Consider Before Ordering an Online DNA Test," by Jane Tiller and Paul Lacaze, The Conversation, 04/05/2018. https://theconversation.com/five-things-to-consider-before-ordering-an-online-dna-test-92504. Licensed Under CC BY-ND 4.0 International.

than genetics, like diet, weather and pollution, also have a big impact on our skin.

Vinome

The pitch: Promoted by Helix, a sort of app store for DNA products, this company says it will curate wines for you on the basis of your DNA.

The price: You have to get an $80 DNA test done through Helix, and then purchase the Vinome profile for $29.99. Vinome says it uses "10 genetic markers related to smell and taste" to identify eight unique profiles, but it also asks you to take a taste preference survey. The company then wants to sell you wine—individual bottles or a membership program—after you get your results.

The science: Researchers have found that certain people are predisposed to hate the taste of brussels sprouts or cilantro, but your inclination for certain wines is probably a lot more complex.

SpareRoom

The pitch: The company makes a mobile app that helps you find a roommate. But it's piloting a new service that uses a DNA sample and an online personality test to match you to a compatible one.

The price: After you submit a spit sample, SpareRoom gives you a report that shows how your genetics influence 14 characteristics, like spontaneity, optimism, stress tolerance, self-awareness, and confidence. The company hasn't yet set the price it will charge when it rolls out the service in the US and UK.

The science: While studies have found genetic links to mental and personality disorders, experts disagree on how much of our character and temperament is actually influenced by our DNA.

The problem with these tests and their ilk, experts say, is that we just don't know enough about the complex interactions of our genes yet to make these kinds of personalized recommendations.

So, why market these services as DNA tests when DNA information can't yet be harnessed to make personalized recommendations?

"When a new area of science emerges that's hot and sexy, it becomes a marketing tool," says Debra Mathews of the Johns Hopkins Berman Institute of Bioethics. As she points out, a similar fad popped up during the heyday of stem cell research: beauty companies started marketing all sorts of "regenerative" skincare products that claimed to contain stem cells.

Beyond the quick buck, though, many of the companies are also playing a long game. Once they sell customers' data, they can compile it and sell it to researchers (for the record, SkinGenie says it doesn't). That's where there's real money to be made.

"I certainly don't think you want to relinquish the rights to your genetic information to get this advice," Mathews says. Her advice before swabbing or spitting: "Read the fine print."

> "The US should enact pre- and post-test genetic counseling requirements by certified professionals and promulgate standardized laboratory and methodological requirements to ensure clinical and analytical validity of the results."

The United States Needs to Regulate Direct-to-Consumer DNA Testing

Sarah F. Sunderman

In the following excerpted viewpoint, Sarah F. Sunderman argues that government regulation is important for customer protections regarding DNA testing companies. The author uses Germany as a model, maintaining that the German government only allows physicians to order DNA tests. There is no ability for direct-to-consumer testing kits to be sold. She also advocates for regulation of DNA testing so consumers fully understand the results they receive from certified experts and so results are generated in a standard and approved fashion. Sarah F. Sunderman is a legislative analyst in the Minnesota House Research Department, Minneapolis. She received her JD degree from Washington University in St. Louis, Missouri.

Sarah F. Sunderman, The Need for Regulation of Direct-to-Consumer Genetic Testing in the United States: Assessing and Applying the German Policy Model, 12 Wash. U. Global Stud. L. Rev. 357 (2013). Available at: https://openscholarship.wustl.edu/law_globalstudies/vol12/iss2/9. This Article is brought to you for free and open access by the Law School at Washington University Open Scholarship. It has been accepted for inclusion in Washington University Global Studies Law Review by an authorized administrator of Washington University Open Scholarship.

As you read, consider the following questions:

1. What was the stated purpose of the German legislative body in regulating DNA testing?
2. According to this viewpoint, why would a physician-only ordering model not work in the United States?
3. What are the benefits of regulating DNA testing?

With the passage of the Human Genetic Examination Act, Gesetz über genetische Untersuchungen bei Menschen [Gendiagnostikgesetz] ("GenDG"), in 2009, the German government enacted many of these recommendations.[117] The legislation requires genetic testing laboratory accreditation, fully informed consent, and genetic counseling for all genetic testing.[118] Moreover, it makes anonymous paternity tests illegal,[119] prohibits parents from using genetic testing to determine the sex of their unborn children,[120] and prohibits genetic discrimination.[121] The GenDG also establishes the independent Genetic Diagnostic Commission, which develops guidelines and reviews new developments in science and technology.[122] Most importantly for the DTC testing industry, the legislation states that predictive genetic examinations may only be ordered through medical doctors that have specialized genetics training and that provide genetic counseling services.[123] In other words, all potential providers of DTC genetic testing would need to persuade German regulatory authorities that their services provide educational and/or informational products rather than medical or clinical services.[124] The provision, in essence, amounts to a complete ban of DTC genetic testing kits ordered directly by consumers.[125]

The legislation's stated purpose is "to protect human dignity and ensure the individual right to self-determination via sufficient information."[126] According to the Deutsches Referenzzentrum für Ethik in den Biowissenschaften, the GenDG' s requirements for predictive genetic testing are based on the individual right to "informational self-determination"[127] and concerns about genetic discrimination for insurance and employment purposes.[128] Concerns about family conflict, stress due to positive test results, and the danger of "geneticising the living world,"[129] also contributed to the development of the GenDG.[130] The requirement that genetic tests be ordered by physicians aims to prevent the commercialization of genetic tests, to guarantee appropriate consultation prior to genetic testing and the correct interpretation of test results, and to protect the results with medical confidentiality requirements.[131] The GenDG's mandated involvement of qualified genetics health care providers and strict informed consent requirements endeavor to protect consumers of genetic testing from both intrinsic and extrinsic ethical, psychological, and medical consequences.[132]

Despite these admirable goals, many critics believe the German legislation's provisions are misguided and overly paternalistic. It is argued that the GenDG is an overly extreme attempt to control German citizens' access to and use of their own genetic information and is based too heavily on the idea of "genetic exceptionalism."[133] Others argue that the prohibition of employee genetic testing may harm German companies in the international market and may be detrimental to insurance companies.[134] Conversely, some contend that the GenDG has too many loopholes and does not go far enough to regulate the genetic testing industry.[135]

Proactive Regulation of DTC Testing the US: Following Germany's Lead, But Forging a Moderate Path

Considering the questionable validity and utility of DTC genetic tests, combined with the potentially serious negative consequences, the United States should follow Germany's example of proactively regulating DTC genetic testing. Though the GenDG, taken as a whole, may appear overly paternalistic, specifically when considering the provisions on prenatal genetic testing that ban seemingly innocuous testing for fetal sex, the provisions related to predictive genetic testing are positive steps in regulating DTC testing. The legislation does not hamper genetic advances—it still gives people the autonomy to choose predictive genetic testing.[136] The GenDG merely requires the involvement of a physician to ensure fully informed consent and to increase clinical utility of the results.[137]

The United States should, through a single regulatory body (rather than the current fragmented and ineffective regulatory framework), adopt regulations similar to the GenDG, though with some notable differences. Theoretically, the German approach makes sense, but in effect amounts to a total ban of DTC testing.[138] Requiring the involvement of physicians specializing in genetics would likely be problematic and could severely limit an individual's ability to undergo genome-wide genetic testing.[139] Therefore, rather than adopting a physician-only approach to DTC testing, the US should enact pre- and post-test genetic counseling requirements by certified professionals and promulgate standardized laboratory and methodological requirements to ensure clinical and analytical validity of the results.[140] Because empirical results are inconclusive as to negative effects, the United States should not completely preclude the possibility of DTC predictive genetic testing and individual choice to pursue that avenue.[141] Concerns about individual autonomy and the right to access one's own genetic information persist, so it is doubtful that a complete ban of DTC genetic testing would be politically feasible in this country.

Since 2012, several DTC testing companies have moved to a physician only business model, as prescribed in the German legislation and most policy recommendations.[142] Most physicians, however, lack specialized knowledge of genetics and genetic testing.[143] Physicians may be ill equipped to fully inform patients about genome-wide predictive genetic testing.[144] Since genetic testing capabilities have progressed rapidly, resulting in a shortage of genetics specialists, state boards and medical associations should institute continuing physician education programs to encourage effective physician involvement in the DTC genetic testing process.[145] To that end, the National Human Genome Research Institute has called for enhanced genetics education in undergraduate and graduate medical programs, as well as continuing professional education.[146] At this point in time, however, requiring the involvement of physicians specializing in genetics would be problematic and may severely limit an individual's ability to undergo genome-wide genetic testing.[147] Mandating physician involvement would likely fail to solve the problems of misinformation and uninformed consent, while restricting individual access.[148]

Balancing the need to combat these problems with the desire for personal autonomy, requiring genetic counseling for all DTC tests seems to be the best solution. The American Medical Association emphasized the importance of genetic counseling in their February 2011 letter to the FDA.[149] By mandating quality, thorough genetic testing, the US regulatory body would continue to allow people to access their genetic information, while ensuring that they can fully understand it and cope with it.

[...]

Conclusion

As genome-wide predictive testing becomes more integrated into the health care scheme,[157] DTC testing will only become more prominent if left unregulated. Some argue that this would be a positive development for personalized medicine, prevention, genetic education and awareness, and individual autonomy to access one's own genetic information.[158] However, considering the many ethical concerns and possible negative consequences of predictive DTC genetic testing, such as lack of clinical and analytical validity, possible psychological strain, and little clinical utility,[159] it is in the United States' interest to limit the unfettered growth of this industry. Germany heeded the advice of countless international medical and genetics organizations and enacted legislation that protects consumers from the possible harms of unregulated predictive genetic testing. The United States should follow Germany's example by requiring satisfactory genetic counseling and enacting standardized laboratory procedure requirements.[160] However, for practical reasons and in order to maintain the autonomy that DTC testing gives consumers, the United States should stop short of Germany's physician-only requirement.

Notes

117. See Untersuchungen bei Menschen [Gendiagnostikgesetz—GenDG] [Human Genetic Examination Act], July 31, 2009, Bundesgesetzblatt [BGBI] at 2529 (Ger.) [hereinafter GenDG], available at http://www.eurogentest.org/uploads/1247230263295/ GenDG_German_English.pdf (contains original German version and English translation).

118. Id. §§ 5, 13.

119. Id. Some misdemeanor violations are punishable by fines up to five thousand euro. Id. § 26(2). Other violations can be punishable with fines of up to five-hundred thousand euro. Id.

120. Id. § 15(1) ("A prenatal genetic examination may only be conducted for medical purposes and to the extent it is targeted at determining certain genetic characteristics of the embryo or foetus which, according to the generally accepted status of science and technology, might impair its health before or after birth or if treatment of an embryo . . . .") (emphasis added). The section goes on to say that if a fetus's sex is determined during medical prenatal testing, the parents may find out the results.

121. Id. § 1. The GenDG prohibits employers and insurance companies from demanding genetic testing of employees and individuals, subject to narrow exceptions.

122. Id.

123. Id. After having received written information on the contents of the counseling, an individual may waive their right to genetic counseling in writing. Id. § 10. Additionally, after counseling, the person concerned shall be allowed adequate time for consideration before undergoing the test. Id.

124. David Clark, Genetic Exceptionalism and Paternalism Themes in New German Legislation, GENOMICS L. REP. (Sept. 2, 2009), available at http://www. genomicslawreport.com/index.php/2009/ 09/02/genetic-exceptionalism-and-paternalism-themes-in-new-german-legislation/.

125. Id.

126. GenDG, supra note 116, § 1.

127. See Birte Herrfurth-Rödig et al., Predictive Genetic Testing, GER. REF. CTR. FOR ETHICS IN THE LIFE SCI. [DRZE] (Nov. 2011) (Ger.), available at http://www.drze. de/in-focus/predictive-genet ic-testing.

Genetic data can touch upon the core areas of an individual's personality. It can therefore be considered to be generally accepted that as far as their own genetic constitution is concerned every individual is entitled to a "right to know" as well as a "right not to know." Both are commonly subsumed under the concept of "informational self-determination." Problems arise in cases where one person's right not to know collides with another person's right to know. Id.

128. Id.

129. Id. (available at http://www.drze.de/in-focus/predictive-genetic-testing/ethical-aspects). "Geneticising" refers to the reduction of individuals solely to their DNA. Id.

130. Id.

131. Id.

132. Id.

133. Clark, supra note 124. Genetic exceptionalism is "the belief that genetic information is qualitatively different from other forms of personal or medical information." Id.; see also Caroline Wright, Update on Genetic Non-Discrimination Legislation, PHG FOUNDATION (Aug. 10, 2009), http://www.phgfoundation.org/news/4752/.

134. See, e.g., Peter Singer, German Genetics Law a Double-Edged Sword, JAPAN TIMES (July 18, 2009), available at http://www.japantimes.co.jp/text/eo20090718a1.html.

135. See New German Law Restricts Genetic Testing, DEUTSCHE WELLE (Apr. 24, 2009), http://www.dw-world.de/dw/article/0,,4201588,00.html.

136. Id.

137. See Herrfurth-Rödig et al., supra note 127.

138. See Clark, supra note 124.

139. See Heidi Carmen Howard & Pascal Borry, Is There a Doctor in the House? The Presence of Physicians in the Direct-to-Consumer Genetic Testing Context, 3 J. COMMUNITY GENETICS 105, 109 (2012), available at http://www.ncbi.nlm.nih.gov/pmc/articles/PMC3312941/.

140. See Hogarth et al., supra note 41.

141. See, e.g., Cinnamon S. Bloss et al., Direct-to-Consumer Personalized Genetic Testing, 20 HUM. MOL. GENET. R132 (2011), available at http://hmg.oxfordjournals.org/content/early/2011/08/24/ hmg.ddr349.full.

142. See Howard & Borry, supra note 139, at 107–08. For a list of DTC companies now employing the physician-only model, see GPPC List, supra note 1.

143. See Howard & Borry, supra note 139, at 107–08 (pointing out the shortcomings of the physician-only approach and the need for further physician education on genetics). For example, the United Kingdom's National Health Service instituted a program in 2009 to educate physicians on genetics. See NHS Starts Pilot Program to Increase Doctors' Genetics Knowledge, GENOME WEB DAILY NEWS (July 30, 2009), http://www.genomeweb.com/nhs-starts-pilot-program-increase-doctors- genetics-knowledge.

144. Howard & Borry, supra note 139, at 109–11.

145. Id.; see also AM. ACAD. PEDIATRICS, COMM. ON BIOETHICS, Ethical Issues With Genetic Testing in Pediatrics, 107 PEDIATRICS 1451, 1454 (2001), available at http://pediatrics.aappub lications.org/content/107/6/1451.full.pdf ("The number of genetic counselors and geneticists is insufficient for these professionals to take primary responsibility for managing this technology. As a result, primary care physicians will need to expand their knowledge of genetics and the benefits and risks of genetic testing.").

146. Improving Providers' Understanding of Genetic Testing, NAT'L HUMAN GENOME RESOURCE INST., http://www.genome.gov/10002396 (last updated Apr. 2006).

147. Id.

148. Id.

149. AMA to FDA: Genetic Testing Should Be Conducted by Qualified Health Professionals, AMERICAN MED. ASS'N (Feb. 23, 2011), http://www.ama-assn.org/ama/pub/news/news/genetic-test ing-qualified-professionals.page ("Without the benefit of proper medical counseling, patients may spend money on direct to consumer genetic tests needlessly or misinterpret the results of the tests, causing them to make unnecessary or unhealthy lifestyle changes . . . ."); see also FDA Recognizes Role of Genetic Counselors in DTC Testing: A Statement from the National Society of Genetic Counselors, NAT'L SOC'Y GENETIC COUNSELORS (Mar. 9, 2011), http://www.nsgc.org/Portals/0/Press %20Releases/x110309%20Statement%20on%20FDA%20Panel%20 -%20FINALv3%20%20_2_.pdf.

157. See Kenneth P. Tercyak et al., Parents' Attitudes Toward Pediatric Genetic Testing for Common Disease Risk, 127 PEDIATRICS 1288, 1289 (2011), available at http://pediatrics.aappubli cations.org/content/127/5/e1288.full.pdf.

158. See supra Part I, notes 30–41.

159. See supra Part II, notes 42–65.

160. See Press Release, Coll. Am. Pathologists, CAP Urges Increased Oversight of Direct-to-Consumer Laboratory Tests Citing Potential Risk to Patients (July 22, 2010), available at http://www. cap.org/apps/cap.portal?_nfpb=true&cntvwrPtlt_actionOverride=%2Fportlets%2FcontentViewer%2Fs how&_windowLabel=cntvwrPtlt&cntvwrPtlt{actionForm.contentReference}=media_resources%2Fnews rel_direct_to_consumer.html&_state=maximized&_pageLabel=cntvwr. The letter stated that "direct-to-consumer testing is clinical laboratory testing and should be . . . required to meet all applicable requirements as defined by CLIA." Moreover, individuals may need a medical professional to interpret the test results and recommend any future steps or treatment.

> *"HIPAA does not apply to direct-to-consumer genealogy and genetic testing companies like 23andMe and My Heritage, which occupy a legal grey area."*

Privacy Guidelines Do Not Guarantee Consumer Privacy Rights

Tiffany Li and Mason Marks

In the following viewpoint, Tiffany Li and Mason Marks argue that DNA testing companies should adhere to Health Insurance Portability and Accountability Act (HIPAA) regulations to protect consumers' sensitive genetic data. While 23andMe, Ancestry.com, and MyHeritage issued a joint set of privacy best practice guidelines in 2018, the authors still question the real safety of consumer data. Tiffany Li is a visiting fellow at Yale Law School's Information Society Project. Mason Marks is a joint research fellow at New York University Law School and Cornell Tech. He is also a visiting fellow at Yale's Information Society Project.

As you read, consider the following questions:

1. What is the purpose of the Genetic Information Nondiscrimination Act?
2. According to this viewpoint, what are some of the good recommendations made in the testing companies' jointly released privacy guidelines?
3. What company do the authors cite as an example of ineffective privacy policies?

The direct-to-consumer genetic testing industry is booming, and over 12 million people are estimated to have completed testing. Even established companies like weight-loss service Jenny Craig are now offering DNA tests. Last week, amid growing privacy concerns, a group of the largest DNA testing companies, including 23andMe, Ancestry.com, and MyHeritage, jointly released a set of industry best practices regarding user privacy. As DNA testing becomes more mainstream, the question remains: Is your genetic data safe?

The new guidelines arrive on the heels of a string of privacy controversies. Just last month, 23andMe announced a major deal with pharmaceutical giant GlaxoSmithKline, raising concerns about the use of 23andMe users' genetic data in for-profit research. Earlier, 23andMe publicly offered DNA testing services to detained refugees, which sparked outcry from privacy advocates. In May, the National Institutes of Health launched a new initiative seeking the DNA of 1 million Americans. Earlier this year, police used public DNA databases such as GEDmatch to catch criminals including the Golden State Killer.

Industry best practices are a positive step in the right direction, and the new guidelines contain several good recommendations. For example, they suggest that users be permitted to request that their DNA samples be destroyed, and informed consent should be obtained before genetic data is used for research. However, these non-binding, self-imposed guidelines may be insufficient to protect consumer privacy. Consider, for example, the recent Facebook controversies. For years, Facebook promised it would fix the company's privacy problems. Nevertheless, a series of high-profile scandals involving the social media giant have emerged. By comparison, the privacy harms for the genetic testing industry could be far worse. Genetic information is the most intimate personal data that a person can reveal, and the full extent of the privacy risks remain unknown. Moreover, unlike social media, genetic testing has an air of "medicalness" that engenders a false sense of security in consumers.

Current US health privacy laws provide inadequate protection. For instance, the Health Information Portability and Accountability Act protects patient medical information; If doctors or hospitals share health data inappropriately, they can face hefty fines imposed by the Department of Health and Human Services. However, HIPAA does not apply to direct-to-consumer genealogy and genetic testing companies like 23andMe and My Heritage, which occupy a legal grey area. These companies could share users' genetic data with third parties without violating federal law. With only these companies' privacy policies and the new industry guidelines to protect them, consumers of genetic testing services are placing their health data at risk.

If users' genetic information is shared, sold, or stolen, few if any laws protect them from harm. The Genetic Information Nondiscrimination Act prohibits employers and health insurance companies from requesting genetic test results or discriminating against people based on that data. But it has significant limitations. For instance, though it applies to employers and health insurance companies, it does not apply to other entities with an interest in your genetic information such as life insurance companies, lenders, and advertisers. According to Ellen Wright Clayton, a genetics expert and professor of law and medicine at Vanderbilt University, "GINA actually provides very little protection."

Some US lawmakers have taken an interest in the privacy policies of consumer genetic testing companies. If these companies want to continue operating without federal regulation, they need to be more proactive: In addition to agreeing to broad principles like those found in the newly released guidelines, companies should pledge to comply with HIPAA guidelines for the storage and protection of medical information even though they are not required to do so. They should vow to protect not only the raw genetic data that they collect from consumers but also any inferences that can be drawn from that data. They should also consider making all services exclusively opt-in, including participation in research, even if only aggregate data is used. Finally, companies could promise to act as fiduciaries of user information, which would establish duties owed to consumers on par with those characteristic of the trusted relationships between doctors and patients or lawyers and their clients.

Professor Jack Balkin of Yale Law School suggests treating companies that handle large volumes of consumer data as "information fiduciaries" to reduce the risk of consumer exploitation. The concept is gaining traction; it was raised during Mark Zuckerberg's Congressional hearing in April and made its way into India's proposed personal data protection law.

By creating new industry standards specifically aimed at protecting consumer privacy rights, genetic testing companies are asking consumers to trust them. But trust must be earned. Though the guidelines are a good opening statement in an ongoing conversation with consumers, actions speak louder than words. If companies wish to mollify the fears of consumers and regulators, they must do more to protect genetic privacy. Poorly handling user privacy cost Facebook billions this week. If genetic testing companies don't set a better example, their profits could be next to fall.

"Proliferation of such products in the absence of regulation has the potential to damage public trust in accredited and established clinical genetic testing during a critical period of evidence generation for genomics."

Regulation Poses Several Challenges

Jane Tiller and Paul Lacaze

In the following viewpoint Jane Tiller and Paul Lacaze argue that the availability and popularity of direct-to-consumer genetic tests opens the door to misinterpretation and panic. The authors contend that while most such internet-based testing services are based in the United States, other countries such as their home country of Australia should decide how to regulate testing. This will come with challenges, according to the authors, but there are other sectors they can look to. Tiller is a researcher at Monash University in Melbourne, Australia. Lacaze is the Inaugural Head of Public Health Genomics at Monash University, Melbourne, Australia.

"Regulation of Internet-based Genetic Testing: Challenges for Australia and Other Jurisdictions," by Jane Tiller and Paul Lacaze, Frontiers in Public Health, February 15, 2018. 6:24. doi: 10.3389/fpubh.2018.00024. https://www.frontiersin.org/articles/10.3389/fpubh.2018.00024/full Licensed under CC BY 4.0 International.

As you read, consider the following questions:

1. Why is it challenging for Australian companies to provide affordable DTC testing services compared to offshore testing companies?
2. What is the concern with providing risk information for untreatable conditions before symptoms have arisen?
3. What do the authors hope to address in their six-step recommendation to the Australian government?

The Internet currently enables unprecedented ease of access for direct-to-consumer (DTC) genetic testing, with saliva collection kits posted directly to consumer homes from anywhere in the world. This poses new challenges for local jurisdictions in regulating genetic testing, traditionally a tightly-regulated industry. Some Internet-based genetic tests have the capacity to cause significant confusion or harm to consumers who are unaware of the risks or potential variability in quality. The emergence of some online products of questionable content, unsupported by adequate scientific evidence, is a cause for concern. Proliferation of such products in the absence of regulation has the potential to damage public trust in accredited and established clinical genetic testing during a critical period of evidence generation for genomics. Here, we explore the challenges arising from the emergence of Internet-based DTC genetic testing. In particular, there are challenges in regulating unaccredited or potentially harmful Internet-based DTC genetic testing products. In Australia, challenges exist for the Therapeutic Goods Administration, which oversees regulation of the genetic testing sector. Concerns and challenges faced in Australia are likely to reflect those of other comparable non-US jurisdictions. Here, we summarize current Australian regulation, highlight concerns, and offer recommendations on how Australia and other comparable jurisdictions might be more proactive in addressing this emerging public health issue.

Introduction

A direct-to-consumer (DTC) genetic test is any DNA test for a medical or non-medical trait that provides interpretation or communication of test results directly to a consumer, rather than via a health professional. DTC genetic tests are often accessed via the Internet without the need for a medical referral, outside of the health system. Sample collection kits can be posted directly to the consumer without involvement from any health professional. Internet-based DTC genetic tests vary in price, quality, and genetic content measured, ranging from "recreational" testing[1] to return of medical disease risk information.[2] Online DTC genetic tests are growing in popularity due to various consumer motivations, many of which are not necessarily medical in nature.[2,3] There are several potential harms and consequences of poorly regulated Internet-based DTC testing, which have been well documented.[4–6]

Online DTC genetic tests are generally delivered in the absence of genetic counseling or medical oversight. Some consumers with DTC test results are now looking to general practitioners or clinical genetic services for assistance with interpretation or management of DTC genetic findings, posing an emerging challenge for the medical community.[6,7]

Many online DTC genetic tests originate in the USA, where the Food and Drug Administration (FDA) has ongoing challenges in maintaining regulatory oversight.[8] Online DTC tests originating from the USA under FDA approval do not necessarily obtain country-specific approval elsewhere in non-US jurisdictions. However, many are still available and accessible via the Internet from any country, essentially by-passing local testing regulations in non-US countries. Some online DTC tests, if sold locally in non-US jurisdictions, would be in violation of local guidelines for genetic testing. However, direct access via a global online marketplace creates challenges for non-US authorities in enforcing local regulations on Internet-based products.

How local jurisdictions, such as Australia, the UK, and Europe, should approach regulation and quality control of Internet-based genetic testing is uncertain.[9–12] The immediate availability and direct nature of access pose new challenges. Although difficult, many of these challenges are not necessarily unique to the field of genetic testing and have been mirrored in other regulated industries recently disrupted by the emergence of a global online marketplace, such as the online prescription drug sector.[13]

Current Regulation of Genetic Testing in Australia

Under current Australian regulation, there is a strict regulatory regime governing the registration and provision of human genetic tests offered by Australian companies.[14–17] Furthermore, laboratories which carry out genetic testing must be accredited for technical competencies by the National Association of Testing Authorities.[18] These standards mandate a level of quality control for genetic testing services in Australia. However, compliance with these standards makes it challenging, and relatively expensive, for Australian companies to provide price-competitive DTC testing services compared with offshore DTC companies. Such offshore companies can access Australian consumers via the Internet, but are not subject to any Australian regulation.

Consumers may have difficulty distinguishing between locally accredited Australian products and unaccredited, offshore products marketed online. The inability of local authorities such as the Therapeutic Goods Administration (TGA) to regulate online DTC genetic testing and advertising leads to a multitude of regulatory, medical, and ethical concerns, which are set out below and summarized in Table 1. In addition, Australian regulation explicitly allows consumers to access non-accredited overseas tests through a self-importation exemption[14] [Reg 7.1 and Schedule 4].

Table 1. Concerns with unaccredited online direct-to-consumer (DTC) genetic testing.

REGULATION/ QUALITY	Challenging for local authorities to regulate online products No technical standards for quality control No scientific standards for evidence of significance or actionability
MEDICAL	Return of actionable genetic findings without medical oversight DTC customers seek interpretation from local health services Potentially damaging to the reputation of medical genomics
ETHICAL	Return of actionable genetic findings without genetic counseling Disclosure of risk variants for non-treatable conditions Erosion of informed consent Recreational intent versus unintended genetic findings
PRIVACY	DTC companies retain consumer data and DNA samples Access to genetic data by third parties, without consumer consent

Concerns with Unaccredited Internet-Based DTC Genetic Tests

Regulation/Quality

Although stringent standards apply to genetic testing conducted in Australia, the TGA and other regulators are not empowered to prevent access to or regulate the quality of Internet-based DTC genetic tests conducted overseas. Similar issues are faced by other international regulators,[9] with issues reported such as difficulties determining whether DTC samples were being processed locally or sent overseas.[11] Given the challenges of genomic literacy in the general population,[19, 20] many consumers may not be aware of the quality of online genetic tests. Thus, consumers are vulnerable to online marketing by overseas companies, especially for some of the more questionable products generally opposed by the scientific and medical community.[10, 21]

Medical Issues

There is evidence consumers of Internet-based genetic tests are increasingly seeking the advice of general practitioners or clinical genetics services for interpretation of results.[22] This risks placing an increased burden on existing local health services, which are often publicly funded with limited resources. Funding of additional services to accommodate a growing influx of DTC consumers may not be sustainable in Australia and other comparable nations,[23] particularly when results can be ambiguous, uncertain, or confusing, and often identified in individuals not at genuinely increased risk of disease. With some Internet-based DTC companies returning significant genetic risk information of medical and psychological gravity, such as variants in the BRCA genes, without any genetic counseling or medical support, there is also scope for potential harm[24] and/or inadequate care for those who need it.

Furthermore, consumers may have difficulty in distinguishing between established locally accredited clinical genetic testing services (meeting high standards of quality control), versus cheaper online options not subject to the same quality measures. This has the potential to confuse consumers and may compromise long-standing efforts of local genetic services.[25]

Ethical Issues

Consumers purchasing DTC genetic tests may be motivated by curiosity, ancestry, or recreational motivations rather than medical reasons. However, they may uncover serious medical risk factors, non-paternity, or other unexpected genetic information in the process of testing, without having considered the implications beforehand.[5, 26] In addition, some online tools can now be used to analyze raw genetic data from non-medical DTC tests (such as ancestry tests), to generate interpretations of medical risk. This means individuals can now access medical risk information from raw genetic data online, without any regulation, quality control, or medical oversight after undertaking an ancestry test. This opens up the potential for incorrect interpretation as well as the return of genuinely medically significant risk information without informed consent, genetic counseling, or medical oversight.[27]

Genetics services providing clinical testing in Australia follow international guidelines regarding the evidence required to substantiate medical risk information before it is provided to the consumer.[28] Model guidelines have also been developed for the evaluation of genetic tests,[29] but online DTC companies can provide medical risk information to consumers without fulfilling these evidence requirements.[30] Informed consent for Internet-based DTC products does not meet traditional clinical genetic standards, with most DTC companies currently not providing pre- or post-test genetic counseling or medical support.[10]

Some DTC tests return genetic risk information for untreatable conditions prior to symptom onset, such as the APOEe4 risk allele of Alzheimer's disease.[31] Although some studies have shown such results can be used by at-risk individuals to plan ahead,[3] direct provision of this information without access to genetic counseling or medical oversight is generally not standard practice in the clinical genetics community, and is considered by many to be unethical.[32] Media reports have detailed anecdotes of individuals who have unexpectedly received risk information for Alzheimer's disease through DTC testing and experienced distress as a result.[33]

Privacy Issues

The increasing number of consumers providing DNA samples to online companies also raises concerns around the privacy of genetic data. Recent studies have shown that many online DTC companies do not consistently meet international guidelines regarding data use and privacy,[34] and consumers' expectations around privacy and use of their genetic data can be inconsistent with companies' practices.[35] Many online DTC companies retain DNA samples for subsequent use, including research, with potentially ambiguous consumer information about the use and storage of DNA samples.[36] Furthermore, it has been suggested that online DTC companies are selling access to their databases of genetic information to third parties, or providing samples for research purposes, potentially without the knowledge or consent of consumers who provided the data.[34, 35]

Future Considerations and Recommendations

Given the growing fascination with genetic testing, it is inevitable consumers will continue to seek Internet-based DTC products. The demand for cheap, Internet-based DTC genetic testing may also be fueled by the lack of access to, and cost of, locally accredited clinical genetic testing options in some countries, especially those with publicly funded health systems.[37]

There is currently no international association tasked with regulating the online DTC market. The Global Alliance for Genomics and Health[38] is developing standards for the sharing of genomic data, but does not have regulatory powers. The limited amount of public funding allocated for clinical genetic testing in most countries, combined with the increased demand for clinical genetic testing, means many individuals who do not qualify for publicly funded testing under current guidelines may seek alternative, low-cost ways of obtaining genetic information directly.

Unless governments take steps to inform consumers of the dangers of some online DTC genetic testing products, or provide alternative testing pathways, it is likely that consumers will continually have difficulty distinguishing between quality (locally accredited) and non-quality (unaccredited) online products. Many consumers may choose low-priced, low-quality tests and therefore be vulnerable to many of the medical, ethical, and privacy concerns. The potential for confusion, unexpected outcomes, and harm will increase and could threaten the public perception of genomics at a critical time. It is vital that public faith and engagement are safeguarded during the ongoing period of evidence generation for implementation of genomic medicine.

In the future, the concept of governments or public health systems providing access to universal, population-wide genomic screening for disease prevention needs to be considered. This would provide an alternative testing pathway to unregulated Internet-based DTC testing accessed through the private sector. It would ensure stronger quality control, appropriate informed consent, and implementation of evidence-based prevention following national screening principles.[39] A recommendation in this regard is set out below. If publicly funded screening is not implemented, it is likely Australia and other jurisdictions will continue to see consumers gravitate toward cheap, Internet-based genetic testing options, especially when genomic literacy remains low.

We recommend the Australian government and comparable jurisdictions take the following steps:

1. Promote education of the public regarding DTC genetic testing, including publicizing warnings in prominent and widely accessed media about risks of unaccredited online DTC genetic testing products.

2. Publicly endorse any local or international companies whose genetic tests meet local accreditation standards, though an easily recognizable accreditation icon, so that consumers can readily identify valid and approved tests.

3. Amend current regulations so that personal importation of unaccredited genetic tests is not sanctioned.

4. Prohibit Internet advertising of non-accredited offshore tests and engage with overseas regulators regarding strategies for regulating advertising of, and access to, online tests.

5. Implement compulsory guidelines requiring the application of evidence requirements for interpretation of genetic tests before the return of results to consumers.

6. Consider a proof-of-concept study to pilot the development of a low-cost, publicly funded, population genomic screening program for young adults, linked with the health system, accompanied by education, focused on the delivery of evidence-based, medically useful risk information for those who seek it.

The implementation of these recommendations would require significant allocation of resources by the government, both toward regulation of online tests and steps toward building a health system capable of undertaking population genomic screening, including scaling of genetic counseling and other medical services. Significant feasibility studies and health-economic modeling will be required before this can become a reality.

The future landscape of genetic testing in countries with strong public health systems, such as Australia, remains uncertain. Many individuals will continue to seek DTC testing via the online marketplace regardless, especially for recreational purposes such as ancestry testing, which have limited potential for harm. However, for medical risk information, there are more complexities to consider.

The prospect of a national genomic screening program in Australia to identify actionable genetic risk in consenting adults could be considered. This could potentially identify preventable disease risk early, which if linked to public health system services, could enable closer and more appropriate medical, scientific, and ethical oversight for mainstreaming of genomic testing. A public health screening strategy would ensure those genuinely at-risk are identified and offered appropriate clinical genetic services when needed. Under this model, only established actionable genetic findings, supported by clinical guidelines and standard-of-care for preventable disease, would be disclosed (meaning most individuals would not be receiving results). This may make interpretation of genomic results and subsequent medical risk assessments more achievable.

Screening could be accompanied by national education and genomic literacy programs. These efforts may deter people from seeking unaccredited DTC testing products online for medical disease risk assessment and encourage appropriate management for those genuinely at risk. The prospect of genomic population screening linked to a public health system would require significant bolstering of Australian clinical genetic services, far beyond the current scope. This would need substantive increases in public funding and infrastructure. Steps in this direction will need to be considered as the wave of consumers turning to DTC testing will continue to rise in coming years.

The Internet, combined with an increasing public fascination in genomics, is currently resulting in an unprecedented access to genetic testing. This will continue to rise and present new challenges for nations in regulating testing and interpretation services. It is likely a pro-active and forward-thinking approach to regulation will be required.

References

1. Felzmann H. 'Just a bit of fun': how recreational is direct-to-customer genetic testing? New Bioeth (2015) 21(1):20–32. doi:10.1179/2050287715Z.00000000062

2. Covolo L, Rubinelli S, Ceretti E, Gelatti U. Internet-based direct-to-consumer genetic testing: a systematic review. J Med Internet Res (2015) 17(12):e279. doi:10.2196/jmir.4378

3. Roberts JS, Gornick MC, Carere DA, Uhlmann WR, Ruffin MT, Green RC. Direct-to-consumer genetic testing: user motivations, decision making, and perceived utility of results. Public Health Genomics (2017) 20(1):36–45. doi:10.1159/000455006

4. Crawshaw M. Direct-to-consumer DNA testing: the fallout for individuals and their families unexpectedly learning of their donor conception origins. Hum Fertil (2017) 11:1–4. doi:10.1080/14647273.2017

5. Moray N, Pink KE, Borry P, Larmuseau MH. Paternity testing under the cloak of recreational genetics. Eur J Hum Genet (2017) 25(6):768–70. doi:10.1038/ejhg.2017.31

6. van der Wouden CH, Carere DA, Maitland-van der Zee AH, Ruffin MT 4th, Roberts JS, Green RC, et al. Consumer perceptions of interactions with primary care providers after direct-to-consumer personal genomic testing. Ann Intern Med (2016) 164(8):513–22. doi:10.7326/M15-0995

7. Koeller DR, Uhlmann WR, Carere DA, Green RC, Roberts JS, PGen Study Group. Utilization of genetic counseling after direct-to-consumer genetic testing: findings from the impact of Personal Genomics (PGen) study. J Genet Couns (2017) 26(6):1270–9. doi:10.1007/s10897-017-0106-7

8. Curnutte M. Regulatory controls for direct-to-consumer genetic tests: a case study on how the FDA exercised its authority. New Genet Soc (2017) 36(3):209–26. doi:10.1080/14636778.2017.1354690

9. Phillips AM. Only a click away—DTC genetics for ancestry, health, love…and more: a view of the business and regulatory landscape. Appl Transl Genom (2016) 8:16–22. doi:10.1016/j.atg.2016.01.001

10. Rafiq M, Ianuale C, Ricciardi W, Boccia S. Direct-to-consumer genetic testing: a systematic review of European guidelines, recommendations, and position statements. Genet Test Mol Biomarkers (2015) 19(10):535–47. doi:10.1089/gtmb.2015.0051

11. Kechagia S, Mai Y, Vidalis T, Patrinos GP, Vayena E. Personal genomics in Greece: an overview of available direct-to-consumer genomic services and the relevant legal framework. Public Health Genomics (2014) 17(5–6):299–305. doi:10.1159/000366175

12. Skirton H, Goldsmith L, Jackson L, O'Connor A. Direct to consumer genetic testing: a systematic review of position statements, policies and recommendations. Clin Genet (2012) 82(3):210–8. doi:10.1111/j.1399-0004.2012.01863.x

13. Montoya ID, Jano E. Online pharmacies: safety and regulatory considerations. Int J Health Serv (2007) 37(2):279–89. doi:10.2190/1243-P8Q8-6827-H7TQ

14. Therapeutic Goods (Medical Devices) Regulations. Canberra: Australian Government, Department of Health (2002).

15. Therapeutic Goods (Excluded purposes) Specification. Canberra: Australian Government, Department of Health (2010).

16. Therapeutic Goods Act. Canberra: Australian Government, Department of Health (1989).

17. Therapeutic Goods Regulations. Canberra: Australian Government, Department of Health (1990).

18. Commonweatlh of Australia. Memorandum of Understanding between the Commonwealth of Australia and the National Association of Testing Authorities, Australia. (2013).

19. Syurina EV, Brankovic I, Probst-Hensch N, Brand A. Genome-based health literacy: a new challenge for public health genomics. Public Health Genomics (2011) 14(4–5):201–10. doi:10.1159/000324238

20. Hurle B, Citrin T, Jenkins JF, Kaphingst KA, Lamb N, Roseman JE, et al. What does it mean to be genomically literate? National Human Genome Research Institute Meeting Report. Genet Med (2013) 15(8):658–63. doi:10.1038/gim.2013.14

21. Webborn N, Williams A, McNamee M, Bouchard C, Pitsiladis Y, Ahmetov I, et al. Direct-to-consumer genetic testing for predicting sports performance and talent identification: consensus statement. Br J Sports Med (2015) 49(23):1486–91. doi:10.1136/bjsports-2015-095343

22. Brett GR, Metcalfe SA, Amor DJ, Halliday JL. An exploration of genetic health professionals' experience with direct-to-consumer genetic testing in their clinical practice. Eur J Hum Genet (2012) 20(8):825–30. doi:10.1038/ejhg.2012.13

23. Middleton A, Mendes Á, Benjamin CM, Howard HC. Direct-to-consumer genetic testing: where and how does genetic counseling fit? Per Med (2017) 14(3):249–57. doi:10.2217/pme-2017-0001

24. Francke U, Dijamco C, Kiefer AK, Eriksson N, Moiseff B, Tung JY, et al. Dealing with the unexpected: consumer responses to direct-access BRCA mutation testing. PeerJ (2013) 1:e8. doi:10.7717/peerj.8

25. Critchley C, Nicol D, Otlowski M, Chalmers D. Public reaction to direct-to-consumer online genetic tests: comparing attitudes, trust and intentions across commercial and conventional providers. Public Underst Sci (2015) 24(6):731–50. doi:10.1177/0963662513519937

26. Nelson B. The big sell: direct-to-consumer tests promise patients more abundant and accessible information, but potential pitfalls abound. Cancer Cytopathol (2016) 124(1):7–8. doi:10.1002/cncy.21684

27. Kirkpatrick BE, Rashkin MD. Ancestry testing and the practice of genetic counseling. J Genet Couns (2017) 26(1):6–20. doi:10.1007/s10897-016-0014-2

28. Richards S, Aziz N, Bale S, Bick D, Das S, Gastier-Foster J, et al. Standards and guidelines for the interpretation of sequence variants: a joint consensus recommendation of the American college of medical genetics and genomics and the association for molecular pathology. Genet Med (2015) 17(5):405. doi:10.1038/gim.2015.30

29. Haddow J, Palomaki G. ACCE: a model process for evaluating data on emerging genetic tests. In: Khoury M, Little J, Burke W, editors. Human Genome Epidemiology: A Scientific Foundation for Using Genetic Information to Improve Health and Prevent Disease. New York: Oxford University Press (2004). p. 217–33.

30. Trent R. Direct-to-consumer DNA genetic testing and the GP. Aust Fam Physician (2014) 43(7):436.

31. Roberts JS, Christensen KD, Kalia S, Mountain J, Green RC. Direct-to-consumer genetic testing for risk of Alzheimer's disease (AD): the psychological and behavioral impact of APOE genotype disclosure. Alzheimers Dement (2014) 10(4):209. doi:10.1016/j.jalz.2014.04.274

32. Gauthier S, Leuzy A, Racine E, Rosa-Neto P. Diagnosis and management of Alzheimer's disease: past, present and future ethical issues. Prog Neurobiol (2013) 110:102–13. doi:10.1016/j.pneurobio.2013.01.003

33. McKie R. Warnings over shock dementia revelations from ancestry DNA tests. The Guardian. (2017).

34. Laestadius LI, Rich JR, Auer PL. All your data (effectively) belong to us: data practices among direct-to-consumer genetic testing firms. Genet Med (2016) 19(5):513–20. doi:10.1038/gim.2016.136

35. Christofides E, O'Doherty K. Company disclosure and consumer perceptions of the privacy implications of direct-to-consumer genetic testing. New Genet Soc (2016) 35(2):101–23. doi:10.1080/14636778.2016.1162092

36. Niemiec E, Howard HC. Ethical issues in consumer genome sequencing: use of consumers' samples and data. Appl Transl Genom (2016) 8:23–30. doi:10.1016/j.atg.2016.01.005

37. Rogowski WH, Grosse SD, Schmidtke J, Marckmann G. Criteria for fairly allocating scarce health-care resources to genetic tests: which matter most? Eur J Hum Genet (2014) 22(1):25–31. doi:10.1038/ejhg.2013.172

38. Global Alliance for Genomics & Health. (2017). Available from: https://www.ga4gh.org/

39. Community Care and Population Health Principal Committee Standing Committee on Screening, Population Based Screening Framework. Adelaide: Australian Health Ministers Advisory Council (2016).

Periodical and Internet Sources Bibliography

The following articles have been selected to supplement the diverse views presented in this chapter.

Association of Corporate Counsel, "Employment Provisions of the Genetic Information Nondiscrimination Act," September 19, 2011. https://www.acc.com/legalresources/quickcounsel/gina.cfm.

Sharon Begley, "Before You Send Your Spit to 23andMe, What You Need to Know," Stat, April 7, 2017. www.statnews.com/2017/04/07/what-you-need-to-know-about-23andme-genetic-test/.

Becca Caddy. "It's All in the Genes: Getting to Grips with DNA Testing," Tech Radar, March 11, 2018. www.techradar.com/best/its-all-in-the-genes-getting-to-grips-with-dna-testing.

Ashley Daly, "New Concerns Over In-Home DNA Tests," Kare 11, November 29, 2017. www.kare11.com/article/news/local/new-concerns-over-in-home-dna-tests/89-495698717.

George Doe, "With Genetic Testing, I Gave My Parents the Gift of Divorce," Vox, September 9, 2014. https://www.vox.com/2014/9/9/5975653/with-genetic-testing-i-gave-my-parents-the-gift-of-divorce-23andme.

Maggie Fox, "What You're Giving Away with Those Home DNA Tests," NBC News, November 29, 2017. www.nbcnews.com/health/health-news/what-you-re-giving-away-those-home-dna-tests-n824776.

Kristina Grifantini, "What's Happening to Your DNA Data? Genetic Testing Services Abound, But Consumers Opting to Use Them Should Be Aware of the Pitfalls," IEEE Pulse, November 27, 2017. pulse.embs.org/november-2017/whats-happening-dna-data/.

Xavier Harding, "23andMe, Ancestry, and Other DNA Testing Companies Agree to Better Protect Your Genetic Information," Mic, July 31, 2018. mic.com/articles/190528/23andme-ancestry-and-other-dna-testing-companies-agree-to-better-protect-your-genetic-information#.Bagb5MoZI.

Erika Check Hayden, "Privacy Protections: The Genome Hacker," Nature, May 8, 2013. https://www.nature.com/news/privacy-protections-the-genome-hacker-1.12940.

Patsy Kelly, "News13 Tests the Accuracy of At-Home DNA Tests for Medical Conditions," WBTW News13, July 5, 2018. www.wbtw.com/news/grand-strand/news13-tests-the-accuracy-of-at-home-dna-tests-for-medical-conditions/1285031505.

Madison Mayfield, "What Happens to Your DNA After It's Tested?" Genetic Direction, May 2, 2018. geneticdirection.com/2018/05/02/what-happens-to-your-dna-after-its-tested/.

Evan B. Symon, "Inside the Shady World of DNA Testing Companies," Cracked, December 4, 2017. www.cracked.com/personal-experiences-2522-inside-shady-world-dna-testing-companies.html.

James Vincent, "23andMe and Other DNA-Testing Firms Promise Not to Share Data without Consent," Verge, August 1, 2018. www.theverge.com/2018/8/1/17638680/genetic-data-privacy-consumer-rights-guidelines-23andme-ancestry.

CHAPTER 3

Should DNA Testing Reveal the Consumer's Identity?

Chapter Preface

DNA testing companies state in their service agreements that data will be anonymized, and in that way, consumers' individual data will be protected. However, legal investigators were able to use decades-old crime scene DNA from a suspected killer and match it using an open-access genealogical database. Such practices vilify DNA testing company promises. AncestryDNA, for example, states that it reserves the right to share a test-taker's personal information if it believes the information is necessary for legal reasons. In 2017, it fulfilled nearly three dozen legal requests in 2017. Other testing services make similar claims on their websites, raising a difficult ethical question: Should DNA testing reveal the consumer's identity?

Much as law enforcement has been able to deanonymize consumer identity, so have medical researchers. Medical studies are bound to a set of ethical standards in which researchers agree to release results as aggregated data. But in recent years, these practices have come into question when dealing with genetic data. There is insufficient privacy protection, because study participants could be re-identified at the individual level.

It does not take much, in fact, to deanonymize genetic data. Birth date, gender, and zip code have been successfully used to track an individual. Cell phone records, too, have been effective. Consumers may be led to believe their data will be kept anonymous, but DNA testing companies cannot realistically assure this.

Another way anonymity becomes compromised is in the matching of an individual's results with those of close relatives. Specific cases attest to complete surprise that a half-sibling arises from such a match, creating havoc within the family structure and possibly resulting in permanent damage to that family. Consumers must be aware of what they are agreeing to when their genetic information is compared to others within the testing company's database. On the other hand, DNA data can be instrumental for adoptees to find birth parents, if those parents have participated in DNA testing with the same company.

The following chapter explores several cases of genetic information anonymity and re-identification. Implications prove to be either positive and negative, depending on the situation. The authors of these viewpoints present these situations and call for a range of solutions.

> "*There are also concerns about how DNA data could be used in the future. For example, you can access your phone with your fingerprint but one day your DNA sequence may become your identity.*"

Online Genetic Testing Has a Dark Side

Catriona May

In the following viewpoint Catriona May argues that, while people tend to focus on commercial personal genetic testing as a fun way to learn their ancestry or a way to connect with distant family members, there is a dark side. Some tests can be used to screen for serious medical conditions, something that is normally done under the watch of genetic counselors. Without that support, and the expert interpretation that comes with it, learning one's results can do more harm than good. Other possibly negative implications are incorrect or incomplete data, privacy violations, and impact on future generations. Catriona May is a Melbourne-based writer and editor with a focus in research and education.

As you read, consider the following questions:

1. What has genetic testing been done for in the past?
2. Why does the researcher quoted in the viewpoint believe that the companies' promises to identify ethnic mixes of consumers is spurious?
3. What are some potential risks regarding the ownership of DNA?

Unlucky in love? Perhaps you haven't found your genetic match yet.

Or maybe you're wondering what interests you should encourage your child to follow. DNA testing claims to offer an answer to that, too.

You can even find out what kind of wine you're genetically predisposed to enjoy.

Personal genomic testing, offered as online DNA tests and often sold direct-to-consumer, is exploding worldwide. In Australia, it's most widely used through genealogy websites, which market DNA testing to help you understand your ethnic make-up and discover long-lost relatives.

But there is a darker side to DIY genetic testing, with in-the-know consumers able to source reports on their predisposition to diseases like Alzheimer's or breast cancer, without any medical advice or support.

Recently, the NextGen home test kit, which markets itself as a way to screen for serious medical conditions in babies and children, came under fire from the Royal College of Pathologists of Australasia for the test taking place "without parents having had a discussion with their doctor, prior to the test being done."

So what do Australians think about personal genomics and what should they be wary of?

These are some of the questions the Genioz study, at the Murdoch Children's Research Institute (MCRI) is seeking to answer. Its team of researchers from several institutes and universities have gathered the views of over 3000 Australians through focus groups, an online survey and forums.

We caught up with lead researcher Professor Sylvia Metcalfe and research assistant Chriselle Hickerton, who are both based at MCRI and the University of Melbourne, to find out more about this growing area.

Can I Get a Genetic Health Report Online, Without Going to the Doctor?

Professor Metcalfe: Traditionally, genetic testing has been done for clinical reasons, usually when someone presents with symptoms or a family history of an inherited disease, like Huntington's disease, or some forms of breast cancer.

But now you can go online and do broader testing that looks at genetic variants throughout the entire genome—DIY genetic testing.

At the moment there are no companies based in Australia offering these tests, but some companies in Asia and Europe do and you can access them online without a doctor's referral.

Ms Hickerton: Or people sometimes use the results from, say, an ancestry test, to then seek a separate report on their health.

They download that raw data which goes to a third-party site and they then get a health information report that comes with risk estimates for various conditions. But some interpretation is usually needed.

It's quite complex and without support from a health professional, like a genetic counsellor, people may not understand their results, as well as any implications, and so may not act appropriately.

How Reliable Are DNA Reports from Ancestry Companies?

Ms Hickerton: While they promise you can "discover your ethnic mix" by submitting a sample of your DNA, their reports can be inaccurate.

Some studies show that, in some isolated populations, patterns of DNA from certain ethnic groups can be identified, but to take DNA data and report a breakdown of someone's ethnicity, without knowing anything else about them, is spurious.

Ancestry companies like ancestry.com.au or 23andme.com use the same technology as clinical genetic tests. They base their reports on patterns in their own population databases and those databases are growing and becoming more accurate as more people complete the tests, accompanied with comprehensive family tree information.

And false results can happen; matching familial genomes is very complicated, particularly as relationships become more distant.

Should I Be Worried About My DNA Data Getting into the "Wrong" Hands?

Professor Metcalfe: A lot of people making their DNA data available online, mainly through ancestry sites, don't realise that it doesn't belong just to them; it also belongs to their family.

We share 50 per cent of our genome with our parents and siblings, and 25 per cent with our aunts, uncles and grandparents.

That data can end up in all sorts of places.

Some companies will sell de-identified data to other companies for research and development purposes, What's unclear is what happens to that data if a company folds or is bought by another company.

There are also concerns about how DNA data could be used in the future. For example, you can access your phone with your fingerprint but one day your DNA sequence may become your identity.

There's also the potential for genetic discrimination or, in a far-fetched scenario, for stolen DNA to be placed at a crime scene so the real culprits avoid prosecution.

But these issues were not a major concern for most people in our study.

Will Following the Advice Offered by a Genomic Wellness Test Make a Significant Impact on My Health?

Ms Hickerton: A significant minority of our participants had completed genomic wellness tests.

These are often ordered through practitioners like naturopaths or nutritionists and they promise clients a personalised prescribed diet and exercise regimen, based on their unique genetic make-up.

We found these sites sometimes make big promises about people's health that they are unlikely to deliver on. Tests tend to be expensive, particularly when combined with consultation fees and supplement purchases.

There is some good science underpinning these tests. There are some genetic variants that mean our metabolic profiles vary, but we need to be careful because so many health outcomes are due to environmental factors and are not pre-determined by our DNA.

Professor Metcalfe: Often reports are based on individual genetic variants that can have opposite effects and some participants said they didn't know what to do with that information.

If practitioners don't have a genomics background, their interpretation of test results may not be accurate and often the advice offered is quite common sense—like exercise regularly, eat less sugar and eat more vegetables.

We found people who do these tests are searching for answers they haven't been able to find in conventional medicine. They may be experiencing chronic unwellness or symptoms that are difficult to pinpoint, like fatigue or headaches.

But often, the biggest benefit people reported was having someone talking to them and taking their symptoms seriously, rather than being told "it's all in your head."

> *"Privacy advocates are still concerned that these companies leave the door open to sharing a customer's genetic information with law enforcement."*

Finding the Golden State Killer Raised Privacy Concerns

Rebecca Robbins

In the following viewpoint, Rebecca Robbins argues that law enforcement used DNA collected from a crime scene to find a genetic match using a genealogy web site. While this tactic cracked the dormant case and identified the Golden State Killer, it also raises serious privacy concerns over third-party use of DNA data collected by testing companies, including 23andMe, Ancestry, MyHeritage, FamilyTreeDNA, and GEDMatch. Saliva samples or cheek swabs are necessary for DNA testing with some companies. The investigators did not have these. But GEDMatch allowed other forms of DNA, enabling the match to the suspected killer's relatives. Rebecca Robbins is a life sciences reporter covering California's Silicon Valley to San Francisco's Mission Bay.

"The Golden State Killer Case Was Cracked with A Genealogy Web Site," by Rebecca Robbins, STAT, April 26, 2018. Reprinted by permission.

As you read, consider the following questions:

1. Why was an open-source genealogy site useful to solve this crime?
2. Why does 23andMe, for example, refuse to respond to law enforcement inquiries?
3. In 2017, how many law enforcement requests did Ancestry find to be valid and how many did it fulfill?

The identity of one of California's most notorious serial killers had been a mystery for decades—until this week, when law enforcement arrested a suspect. Investigators revealed on Thursday that they made the breakthrough using a remarkable tool: a genealogy website.

The unusual manner in which the Golden State Killer case was cracked has sparked wonderment—as well as privacy concerns about how law enforcement can and does use the genetic information that consumers give up to genetic testing companies. That's because companies generally say on their websites that a customer's genetic information can be shared with law enforcement if demanded with a warrant.

Details about exactly what happened in the Golden State Killer investigation remain murky, but here's what's known: Investigators took DNA collected years ago from one of the crime scenes and submitted it in some form to one or more websites that have built up a vast database of consumer genetic information.

The results led law enforcement to the suspected killer's distant relatives, who were presumably among the millions of consumers who have paid up and mailed in a spit kit to track down long-lost family members, learn more about their ancestry, or gauge their risk for medical conditions. That created a pool of potential suspects under the same family tree that investigators eventually narrowed down to 72-year-old former police officer Joseph James DeAngelo, the Sacramento Bee and other news outlets reported.

The lead investigator on the case, Paul Holes, told The Mercury News that his team relied most heavily on GEDmatch, a free open-source website that pools together genetic profiles uploaded by users seeking to conduct research or fill in gaps in their family trees. GEDmatch's database can be accessed without a court order. (GEDmatch was not approached by law enforcement, the site said in a statement to users who log in.)

Holes's comments don't preclude the possibility that investigators may have also used commercial sites.

Three of the leading companies—23andMe, Ancestry, and Family Tree DNA—all said they were not involved in the Golden State Killer investigation. Motherboard reported the same thing about MyHeritage.

A spokesperson for the Sacramento County District Attorney's office confirmed the Sacramento Bee's reporting, but declined to answer questions about which genealogy sites were used. The DA spokesperson also wouldn't say whether law enforcement relied on any voluntary or involuntary cooperation from the companies behind the sites.

Some sites require consumers to send in a sample of saliva or cells swabbed from inside their cheeks—something that investigators in the Golden State Killer case presumably would not have had from a decades-old crime scene. Other sites like GEDmatch, however, allow users to simply upload raw genetic data in the form of endless A's and C's and G's and T's—a process that hypothetically could have allowed investigators to get the information they needed without getting cooperation from companies.

Privacy advocates are still concerned that these companies leave the door open to sharing a customer's genetic information with law enforcement. They say that doing so represents Orwellian state overreach and worry that customers may not realize what they're agreeing to—or, even worse, that the imperfect technology involved puts innocent people at risk. Privacy advocates have also raised concerns about genetic testing sites that sell purportedly anonymized genetic data to third parties, typically to drug makers. Those data, they fear, could ultimately wind up in law enforcement's hands.

All of that is a big part of why several states have put limits on how authorities can conduct familial DNA searches, or banned them entirely.

Here's a breakdown of some of leading companies' policies and histories when it comes to efforts by law enforcement to crack a case.

23andMe

"Under certain circumstances, your information may be subject to disclosure pursuant to a judicial or other government subpoena, warrant or order, or in coordination with regulatory authorities." — company website

The best-known company in the space has received five requests for user data, covering six different accounts, from law enforcement and other US government authorities. It has complied with none of them, according to a report on the company's website last updated in December.

23andMe has said its policy is to resist law enforcement inquiries in order to protect customer privacy, and that it has never given customer information to law enforcement officials. The company doesn't allow users to submit genetic data processed by a third party to turn up long-lost family members in the 23andMe database.

Ancestry

"We may share your Personal Information if we believe it is reasonably necessary to … comply with valid legal process (e.g., subpoenas, warrants)." — company website

In a remarkable 2014 incident, Ancestry revealed to police the identity linked to a DNA sample to comply with a search warrant.

The case involved the 1996 rape and murder of an 18-year-old woman. One killer was convicted and sentenced to life in prison in 1998, but the police department in Idaho Falls, Idaho, still believed there was another person involved. Police came to Ancestry demanding the name of a person that matched the DNA, but the information that the company provided ultimately did not produce a match. (That information came from a publicly available database that Ancestry has since shuttered.)

Since then, Ancestry has said it received no legal requests for genetic information that it deemed valid in 2015, 2016, and 2017, and therefore did not disclose any such information to law enforcement.

In 2017, the company received 34 law enforcement requests for non-genetic user information that it deemed valid. It provided information in response to 31 of those 34 requests, all of which involved investigations into credit card misuse and identity theft, according to a company report.

Family Tree DNA

"We also may be required to disclose an individual's personal information in response to a lawful request by public authorities, including to meet national security or law enforcement requirements." — company website

The company's database played a key role leading to the 2015 arrest of a murder suspect in Phoenix.

An independent genealogy consultant assisted police with their investigation by using a suspected killer's DNA profile to tap at least one database. She wrote in a 2014 email that only Family Tree DNA had a particular marker test from a certain region in the profile, according to public records first reported by the Arizona Republic. The genealogist ultimately helped turn up the suspect's last name, prompting authorities to look closer.

MyHeritage

"MyHeritage will not disclose any of your personal information except … if required by law, regulatory authorities, legal process or to protect the rights or property of MyHeritage or other users." — company website

MyHeritage is among the sites that allow users to upload DNA data processed by another company or provider. That service, of course, is meant only for people uploading their own personal DNA data—not authorities looking to nab a criminal.

GEDmatch

"While the results presented on this site are intended solely for genealogical research, we are unable to guarantee that users will not find other uses." — company website

Unlike most of the other leading sites, GEDmatch doesn't run a business that charges customers for processing a spit kit or cheek swab and uploading the genetic profile into the company database. The site identified as key to cracking the Golden State Killer case is essentially run by users and volunteers. And although the ostensible purpose of the site is for researchers and family historians to draw comparisons and find leads, there are few protections against law enforcement or other third parties from using the pooled data however they please.

In the message to posted users following the breakthrough in the Golden State Killer case, the site said: "It is important that GEDmatch participants understand the possible uses of their DNA, including identification of relatives that have committed crimes or were victims of crimes."

And the site's privacy policy urges anyone requiring "absolute privacy and security" not to upload their genetic data in the first place. "If you already have it here," the site warns, "please delete it."

*"Promises made by companies not
to share personally identifiable
information are meaningless when
it's so easy to re-identify someone."*

There Is No Such Thing as Anonymous Data

Olivia Solon

In the following viewpoint, Olivia Solon argues that while companies may promise that consumer data will be anonymized, that really is not possible. Through experts, the author shows that a person can be identified through a combination of date of birth, gender, and zip code or cell phone usage. Location data that is publicly available could be used to pinpoint a person's identity. Therefore, when a database is breached, this causes major privacy concerns. Olivia Solon is editor of tech investigations at NBC News in San Francisco, California. She was formerly senior technology reporter for Guardian US in San Francisco.

"Data Is A Fingerprint": Why You Aren't As Anonymous As You Think Online," by Olivia Solon, Guardian News and Media Limited, July 13, 2018. Reprinted by permission.

As you read, consider the following questions:

1. How many times was the Australian government's "anonymized" data set downloaded?
2. Eighty-seven percent of the US population can be identified through which three pieces of information?
3. According to this viewpoint, how can informed consent be compromised?

In August 2016, the Australian government released an "anonymised" data set comprising the medical billing records, including every prescription and surgery, of 2.9 million people.

Names and other identifying features were removed from the records in an effort to protect individuals' privacy, but a research team from the University of Melbourne soon discovered that it was simple to re-identify people, and learn about their entire medical history without their consent, by comparing the dataset to other publicly available information, such as reports of celebrities having babies or athletes having surgeries.

The government pulled the data from its website, but not before it had been downloaded 1,500 times.

This privacy nightmare is one of many examples of seemingly innocuous, "de-identified" pieces of information being reverse-engineered to expose people's identities. And it's only getting worse as people spend more of their lives online, sprinkling digital breadcrumbs that can be traced back to them to violate their privacy in ways they never expected.

Nameless New York taxi logs were compared with paparazzi shots at locations around the city to reveal that Bradley Cooper and Jessica Alba were bad tippers. In 2017 German researchers were able to identify people based on their "anonymous" web browsing patterns. This week University College London researchers showed how they could identify an individual Twitter user based on the metadata associated with their tweets, while the fitness tracking app Polar revealed the homes and in some cases names of soldiers and spies.

"It's convenient to pretend it's hard to re-identify people, but it's easy. The kinds of things we did are the kinds of things that any first-year data science student could do," said Vanessa Teague, one of the University of Melbourne researchers to reveal the flaws in the open health data.

One of the earliest examples of this type of privacy violation occurred in 1996 when the Massachusetts Group Insurance Commission released "anonymised" data showing the hospital visits of state employees. As with the Australian data, the state removed obvious identifiers like name, address and social security number. Then the governor, William Weld, assured the public that patients' privacy was protected.

Latanya Sweeney, a computer science grad who later became the chief technology officer at the Federal Trade Commission, showed how wrong Weld was by finding his medical records in the data set. Sweeney used Weld's zip code and birth date, taken from voter rolls, and the knowledge that he had visited the hospital on a particular day after collapsing during a public ceremony, to track him down. She sent his medical records to his office.

In later work, Sweeney showed that 87% of the population of the United States could be uniquely identified by their date of birth, gender and five-digit zip codes.

"The point is that data that may look anonymous is not necessarily anonymous," she said in testimony to a Department of Homeland Security privacy committee.

More recently, Yves-Alexandre de Montjoye, a computational privacy researcher, showed how the vast majority of the population can be identified from the behavioural patterns revealed by location data from mobile phones. By analysing a mobile phone database of the approximate locations (based on the nearest cell tower) of 1.5 million people over 15 months (with no other identifying information) it was possible to uniquely identify 95% of the people with just four data points of places and times. About 50% could be identified from just two points.

The four points could come from information that is publicly available, including a person's home address, work address and geo-tagged Twitter posts.

"Location data is a fingerprint. It's a piece of information that's likely to exist across a broad range of data sets and could potentially be used as a global identifier," De Montjoye said.

Particularly for the working population, this is a stalker's dream.

"You move from home to work and back again in fairly regular patterns. Mostly one person who lives at address A and works at address B," said Anna Johnston, a director of consultancy Salinger Privacy.

Even if location data doesn't reveal an individual's identity, it can still put groups of people at risk, she explained. A public map released by the fitness app Strava, for example, inadvertently became a national security risk as it revealed the location and movements of people in secretive military bases.

In 2015, De Montjoye showed that it was possible to identify the owner of a credit card from among the millions of "anonymised" charges just by knowing a handful of that person's purchases.

Armed with only the names and locations of shops where purchases took place, and the approximate dates and purchase amounts, De Montjoye was able to identify 94% of people by looking at just three transactions. This means someone could find an Instagram photo of you having coffee with friends, a tweet about a recent purchase and an old receipt, and they'd be able to match it to your entire purchase history.

Montjoye and others have shown time and time again that it's simply not possible to anonymise unit record level data—data relating to individuals—no matter how stripped down that data is.

"It might have worked in the past, but it doesn't work any more," he said.

ADOPTEE RELATIVES BENEFIT FROM NEW RULES

Children, grandchildren and other relatives of adopted adults can now trace back through their ancestors' lives—helping them to unearth their family history, discover more about their medical background and reach out to long-lost relatives under new rules introduced today.

Previously, only the person adopted and their birth relatives were able to use specialised adoption agencies to help shed light on their family history and make contact with their biological family members.

The new rules will extend this right to all relatives of adopted adults, from children and grandchildren to partners and adoptive relatives, allowing greater openness in adoption while ensuring adopted people have the right to a private, family life.

Children and Families Minister Edward Timpson, who has 2 adopted brothers, said:

- It's right that descendants and other relatives of adopted adults are able to access important information, such as medical records or genetic health conditions, which could impact upon how they live their life today.
- They should also be able to find out about important events from their past, as well as make contact with family members if they wish.
- This positive change will help thousands of people discover their place in history, while keeping important safeguards in place to protect the right to a private family life for those who were adopted.

"Relatives of Adopted Adults Now Able to Trace Family Tree," by Edward Timpson, The National Archives, September 25, 2014. Reprinted by permission.

There's very little that individuals can do to protect themselves from this kind of privacy intrusion.

"Once our data gets out there, it tends to be stored forever," said Arvind Narayanan, a Princeton computer science professor. "There are firms that specialise in combining data about us from different sources to create virtual dossiers and applying data mining to influence us in various ways."

It's possible to reduce your individual digital breadcrumb trail by paying only in cash and ditching your cellphone, but that's not particularly practical.

"If you want to be a functioning member of society you have no ability to restrict the amount of data that's being vacuumed out of you to a meaningful level," said the security researcher Chris Vickery.

It also makes it extremely difficult for the individual to give informed consent about the way their data is collected by any app or service. Promises made by companies not to share personally identifiable information are meaningless when it's so easy to re-identify someone.

"It comes down to good regulation and proper enforcement," said De Montjoye, adding that Europe's General Data Protection Regulation is a "step in the right direction."

"One of the failings of privacy law is it pushes too much responsibility on to the consumer in an environment where they are not well-equipped to understand the risks," said Johnston. "Much more legal responsibility should be pushed on to the custodians [of data, such as governments, researchers and companies]."

De Montjoye remains an optimist, referencing the "enormous potential" of big data, particularly for medical research and social sciences.

He proposes that instead of releasing large data sets, researchers and governments should develop interfaces that allow others to ask questions of the data without accessing the raw files.

"The idea is to not lose control of the data and ensure subjects remain anonymous," he said.

"Privacy is not dead. We need it and we're going to get there."

> *"It's never an individual decision: if I uploaded my information, I'd be exposing the genetic information of my family members—even relatively distant relatives, as in the case of the Golden State Killer—now and in the future."*

It's Impossible to Know the Consequences of Uploading Genetic Information, Now or in the Future

Elizabeth Minkel

In the following viewpoint Elizabeth Minkel argues that uploading DNA to commercial databases carries with it a host of potential risks, not only to the person sharing his or her genetic information but to his or her relatives and descendants. The author admits that sharing DNA can be a good thing, as when reuniting family members and when used by law enforcement. But she cautions that this information could be used in unethical ways, such as informing employers of genetic information—perhaps not now, but in the future. Elizabeth Minkel is an editor at How We Get to Next.

"Your Great-Grandson's Genetic Privacy," by Elizabeth Minkel, How We Get to Next, July 30, 2018. https://howwegettonext.com/your-great-grandsons-genetic-privacy-eac72329535c. Licensed under CC BY-SA 4.0.

As you read, consider the following questions:

1. How did uploading DNA results catch the Golden State Killer?
2. What could happen when current genetic companies with strict privacy conditions go bankrupt according to the viewpoint?
3. What does the author mean when she says she doesn't need to elaborate on the US justice system and systemic bias?

T he Golden State Killer: a relatively recent nickname (he's been known as the "East Area Rapist" and the "Original Night Stalker," amongst other monikers) for a person who is believed to have committed at least 12 murders, 50 rapes, and 100 burglaries in the Sacramento, California area in the 1970s and 80s. As recently as 2016, the FBI was offering a large reward for information that would lead to his capture, but it wasn't until this week, three decades after he terrorized Sacramento, that a suspect, 72-year-old former police officer Joseph James DeAngelo Jr., was arrested.

The capture of a famous alleged serial murderer and rapist would obviously be big news no matter the circumstances, but it was the methods that led to DeAngelo's arrest that has shocked people this past week. Police had the DNA of the suspect for decades, but it was impossible to connect it to anyone who didn't also have a DNA sample in police databases—none of their existing samples matched. But a distant relative sent a sample of their DNA to a database called GEDmatch, and the police were able to connect that sample, and, subsequently, DeAngelo himself, to the DNA of the Golden State Killer. The match was described by Sacramento DA Anne Marie Schubert as finding "the needle in the haystack."

DNA profiling has been used by law enforcement around the world for decades, and the problems and benefits that have emerged over time way are too numerous and varied to go into in any great detail here. And police have tried to use relatives' DNA—in legally dubious ways—to zero in on suspects, like in this case a few years ago, written up in Wired.

Commercial genetic testing services are relatively new, and the big players like 23andme and AncestryDNA don't allow law enforcement access to their records. But GEDmatch, which has more than a million users, allows people to upload their genetic information into a publicly searchable database (it's often used for things like searching out separated family members or adoption information). It's important to clarify here: if you've sent DNA to something like 23andme, the only way it would wind up on GEDmatch is if you put it there. It's essentially a way for the genetic information siloed in places like 23andme and Ancestry to be cross-referenced—and it's easy to see the good that can do, when it comes to something like reuniting family members.

But it's impossible to know the consequences of uploading genetic information to a database like GEDmatch, now or in the future. In a segment on WNYC's "The Takeaway," NYU law professor Erin Murphy, author of *Inside the Cell: The Dark Side of Forensic DNA*, dove into some of the potential consequences of exposing your genetic information this way. It's never an individual decision: if I uploaded my information, I'd be exposing the genetic information of my family members—even relatively distant relatives, as in the case of the Golden State Killer—now and in the future.

It's a bit mindblowing, thinking about the consequences your genetic information in the public record could have for your descendants. You might be confident that you'll never commit a crime, and there's the classic line about privacy concerns: "Who cares if they see my information, I have nothing to hide." But are you willing to make that choice for your great-grandson? It extends far beyond law enforcement, Murphy points out. Are you comfortable telling your great-grandson's employer that he might carry certain genetic markers?

In the interview, Murphy also cites examples of genetic material given with an expectation of privacy and then sold to for-profit companies when the research organizations went bankrupt. It's impossible to predict where your information will go, who will want to use it—and, most importantly, what they'll want it for.

I listened to Anne Marie Schubert, the Sacramento district attorney, on the radio a few evenings ago. The legacy of the Golden State Killer is one of devastation and trauma, that's undeniable. But when the interviewer repeatedly asked about these privacy concerns, she continually brushed them aside with reminders that the suspect in question had caused so much harm that the methods were warranted.

I have sympathy for this perspective, but I also believe that legal systems, when they work well, cannot make exceptions: the same methods that might put a man who deserves it behind bars can be used to falsely arrest and imprison others, especially where individual or systemic bias is involved (and yes, we're talking about the US justice system here, so I probably don't need to spell any of this out). It's easy to think of the benefit this kind of DNA matching has for an individual case—but nothing about DNA is individual.

"It is now possible to take DNA from a supposedly anonymous dataset, find matches in public genetic databases, and then work out the identity of the individual by building a family tree. This might pose a real privacy challenge for people who have donated their DNA in the belief that it would remain anonymous, and that their possibly-serious medical conditions would never be connected with them."

New Capabilities May Discourage People From Allowing the Release of Their DNA for Scientific Research

Glyn Moody

In the following viewpoint Glyn Moody argues that scientists are getting better at identifying individuals through online ancestry sites, thanks to sophisticated techniques and growing databases. Given the fact that people shed DNA wherever they go, samples can be matched to DNA found in DNA-based genealogical sites. The ethical implications are strong: Many people release their DNA anonymously to these sites, intending it to be used for scientific purposes. But science is sophisticated enough to determine identity even on an anonymous sample. Glyn Moody is a freelance journalist who writes and speaks about privacy, surveillance, digital rights, open source, copyright, patents and general policy issues involving digital technology.

As you read, consider the following questions:

1. In what percent of the searches was a match found that corresponded to a relative as close as a second cousin according to the viewpoint?
2. Why does the viewpoint stipulate that the researchers' dataset is not representative of the entire US population?
3. How can scientists build a family tree and identify a person's identity using information found in genetic databases?

Earlier this year, Privacy News Online wrote about how long-standing linked but unsolved murder cases were resolved by checking genetic material found at some of the crime scenes against online DNA-based genealogy sites. The partial matches with others on the database indicated that they were relatives of the murderer. By drawing up a family tree containing some 1000 people, the investigators were able to work out who might be the killer.

The genetic genealogist who played a key role in establishing the identity of the murderer was Barbara Rae-Venter. The *New York Times* has just published a fascinating tale of how Rae-Venter used DNA tests and publicly-available genetic information to establish the identity of a woman who was kidnapped as a child. Once more, Rae-Venter searched DNA-based genealogical sites for rough matches with the victim's DNA. From these, she was ultimately able to establish the kidnapped girl's family tree and thus identity.

The increasingly successful use of this technique raises an important question: given a DNA sample, how likely is it that there will be a rough match among consumer genetics databases? A US-Israeli group of researchers have published a paper exploring exactly that issue, and the results have major implications for privacy.

The researchers used a dataset of 1.28 million individuals who had sent their DNA to be analyzed by one of the increasingly-popular consumer genomics companies such as 23andMe. They took random individuals from this pool, and searched for any distant family members that might also be present in the dataset. Interestingly, they did not look for close relationships, because there is apparently a tendency for near-relatives to get tested together, which would skew the results for finding matches. Distant relatives are less likely to act in a coordinated fashion, and so searching for such matches give a better indication of the true power of this kind of genetic analysis.

In 15% of the searches, a match which corresponded to a second cousin or closer relative was found. In 60% of the searches carried out by the research team, a match which corresponded to a third cousin or closer relative was found. That's significant, because the case involving the unsolved murders mentioned above used matches at this level. The new paper therefore indicates that for around 60% of the genetic pool studied there would be a match that would probably be good enough to identify them if they had left DNA at a location.

However, it's important to note that the dataset used by the researchers was not representative of the US population of a whole. About 75% of the 1.28 million individuals were primarily of North European genetic background. This means that individuals primarily from that background were more likely to have a match than individuals whose genetic background was primarily from sub-Saharan Africa, say. Nonetheless, the figures in the study still give a good idea of how easy it has become to find matches for genetic material in DNA genealogy databases.

The researchers went on to calculate how big the pool of DNA samples would have to be to make the probability of finding a rough match near to certainty. They found that a genetic database needs to cover only 2% of the target population to provide a third cousin match to nearly any person:

> we predict that with a database size of [about] 3 million US individuals of European descent (2% of the adults of this population), over 99% of the people of this ethnicity would have at least a single 3rd cousin match and over 65% are expected to have at least one 2nd cousin match. With the exponential

growth of consumer genomics, we posit that such database scale is foreseeable for some 3rd party websites in the near future.

It may take a little longer, but the same will be true for people who descend from most other ethnic groups. The researchers went on to consider how easy it would be to establish the exact identity of a person of interest after finding one or more distant relatives in a familial search. The group tried to reduce the number of people who would need to be interviewed, using basic demographic information, such as geography, age, and gender:

> On the basis of counting relevant relatives of the match, the initial list of candidates contains on average [about] 850 individuals. Our simulations indicate that localizing the target to within 100 miles will exclude 57% of the candidates on average. Next, availability of the target's age to within [plus or minus five years] will exclude 91% of the remaining candidates. Finally, inference of the biological sex of the target will halve the list to just around 16-17 individuals, a search space that is small enough for manual inspection.

This has important implications for people who have provided their DNA for scientific purposes, and allowed it to be released anonymously. As the researchers go on to show in their paper, it is now possible to take DNA from a supposedly anonymous dataset, find matches in public genetic databases, and then work out the identity of the individual by building a family tree. That's a big problem, because it means that it will be possible to put names to DNA sequences that may have easily-identified medical problems. Clearly, this might pose a real privacy challenge for people who have donated their DNA in the belief that it would remain anonymous, and that their possibly-serious medical conditions would never be connected with them.

That new capability may impact the willingness of people to allow their DNA to be released for scientific research. But there is a broader problem that will affect everyone. The research described above indicates that soon, US individuals of European descent will have lost their genetic anonymity. Those descended from other major populations will find themselves in a similar situation in due course.

Already, given a DNA sample, distant relatives can probably be found. That's the case whether or not the individual concerned had uploaded DNA to a consumer genomics company. And from those close relatives it is likely that a family tree could be built up that would allow them to be correctly identified. Moreover, as more people add their genetic profiles to genealogical databases, the easier, quicker and cheaper it will become to name them.

It is not unreasonable to assume that in a few years' time, there will be well-populated family trees for more or less everyone in countries where consumer genomics is offered as a low-cost service. As a result, for almost any genetic material found on an object, or at a site, it will be possible to establish the likely identity of the person who left it there. Since we are continuously shedding our DNA wherever we go, this could become the perfect way to identify people and to track their movements and activities—without the need to install any surveillance equipment beforehand.

Periodical and Internet Sources Bibliography

The following articles have been selected to supplement the diverse views presented in this chapter.

Kristen V. Brown, "'Everyone Will Be Potentially Identifiable': Booming DNA Testing Means No Identity Is Hidden on the Web," *Bloomberg*, October 11, 2018. https://www.bloomberg.com/news/articles/2018-10-11/with-consumer-dna-boom-data-can-identify-those-who-never-tested.

Kristen V. Brown, "Share Your DNA, Get Shares: Startup Files an Unusual Offering," BenefitsPro, October 5, 2018. www.benefitspro.com/2018/10/05/share-your-dna-get-shares-startup-files-an-unusual/?slreturn=20181126092557.

Sarah Chodosh, "Consumer DNA Tests Can't Tell You Much, But They Sure Can Get Your Relatives Arrested," *Popular Science*, May 2, 2018. www.popsci.com/consumer-dna-tests-golden-state-killer.

Yvonne Colbert, "The Privacy Implications of DNA Testing Kits That Can 'Alter Your Life,'" CBC News, January 31, 2018. www.cbc.ca/news/canada/nova-scotia/dna-testing-privacy-terms-and-conditions-1.4508488.

Rhys Dipshan, "Giving Away Your Genes: U.S. Laws' Blind Spot with DNA Data," *Legal Tech News*, August 2, 2018. www.law.com/legaltechnews/2018/08/02/giving-away-your-genes-u-s-laws-blind-spot-with-dna-data/?slreturn=20181126091214.

Erica Evans, "Is DNA Testing Telling Us More Than We Want to Know? The Untold Story of Ancestry.com," *Deseret News*, May 30, 2018. www.deseretnews.com/article/900018325/is-dna-testing-telling-us-more-than-we-want-to-know-the-untold-story-of-ancestrycom.html.

Matt Ford, "How the Supreme Court Could Rewrite the Rules for DNA Searches," *New Republic*, April 30, 2018. newrepublic.com/article/148170/supreme-court-rewrite-rules-dna-searches.

Carolyn Y. Johnson, "Even If You've Never Taken a DNA Test, a Distant Relative's Could Reveal Your Identity," *Washington Post*, October 11, 2018. www.washingtonpost.com/science/2018/10/11/

even-if-youve-never-taken-dna-test-distant-relatives-could-reveal-your-identity/?noredirect=on&utm_term=.7a4944731c66.

Nicole Karlis, "DNA Testing Companies Put Everyone's Privacy at Risk," *Salon*, October 15, 2018. www.salon.com/2018/10/15/dna-testing-companies-puts-everyones-privacy-at-risk/.

Amy Dockser Marcus, "Researchers Identify Relatives from DNA Data Online," *Wall Street Journal*, October 11, 2018. www.wsj.com/articles/researchers-identify-relatives-from-dna-data-online-1539285736.

Ellen Matloff, "If I'm Adopted, Should I Have DNA Testing?" *Forbes*, July 11, 2018. www.forbes.com/sites/ellenmatloff/2018/07/11/im-adopted-should-i-have-dna-testing/#b2111b7e029f.

Amanda Quintana, "Experts Warn DNA Testing Kits Could Put Your Genetic Information in the Wrong Hands," Channel 3000, March 20, 2018. www.channel3000.com/news/experts-warn-dna-testing-kits-could-put-your-genetic-information-in-the-wrong-hands/718527523.

Malcolm Ritter, "Study: DNA Websites Cast Broad Net for Identifying People," AP News, October 11, 2018. www.apnews.com/308188da734f404e9c2aa5988dd5ba74.

Maya Wei-Haas, "Could DNA Testing Reunite Immigrant Families? Get the Facts," *National Geographic*, June 25, 2018. news.nationalgeographic.com/2018/06/DNA-testing-genetics-migrant-families-separated-children-border-science/.

CHAPTER 4

Should Testing Companies Share Genetic Data with Research Partners?

Chapter Preface

The DNA testing service company 23andMe made headlines in the summer of 2018 when it announced a data sharing partnership with pharmaceutical giant GlaxoSmithKline. Underscoring the agreement is a $300 million investment GSK makes in the Silicon Valley company headed up by Anne Wojcicki, a former Google executive. The announcement raised many concerns about data anonymity and privacy of those 23andMe users who may or may not have carefully read the terms in their service agreements when granting their informed consent. One thing is certain: These users will get none of the profits from their own data.

Drug companies, scientific research endeavors, and governments all seek genetic data for their own purposes. In scientific and university field research, specific standards dictate ethical practices. However, when it comes to DNA information, there is no real regulation, pundits argue, and such regulation must go beyond the Genetic Information Nondiscrimination Act, which prohibits employers from using genetic information about employees and job applicants.

Beyond the legal aspects, some advocates believe consumers should reap financial rewards of their own contributions. A few companies invite test-takers to upload their own DNA to their websites. Open-platform scientific projects such as Harvard's Personal Genome Project do the same. And there are some test-takers who upload their data to their own websites in the name of open-sharing.

At the core of the data sharing debate is whether DNA testing companies are to be trusted and whether their privacy statements hold firm. Also key to the discussion is whether DNA information can be traced back to individuals. While testing companies promise anonymity, legal and scientific researchers have shown genetic data can be de-anonymized.

The following chapter examines the practice and repercussions of DNA data sharing, data mining, and data profiteering. The authors of the viewpoints present opposing opinions on the ethics of data exchange, particularly with third parties, including large pharmaceutical companies.

> *"It would be possible to create genetically targeted bio-weapons that only work against the DNA of one person in particular, while leaving everyone else unharmed. To investigators, the illness or death of one person would simply seem to be due to an unknown factor, or just chance."*

Cataloging Citizens' DNA Would Help Solve Crimes but at a Great Cost to Privacy and Safety

Glyn Moody

In the following viewpoint Glyn Moody argues that the suggestion by some to create national databases of citizens'—and in some cases, visitors' and tourists'—DNA is a slippery slope. The idea that such catalogs would make it easier for law enforcement to solve crimes is fair, but the author lists many horrors that could come along with such convenience. Glyn Moody is a freelance journalist who writes and speaks about privacy, surveillance, digital rights, open source, copyright, patents, and general policy issues involving digital technology.

"It's coming: another call for everyone's DNA to be collected and stored permanently," by Glyn Moody, Privacy News Online, May 16, 2017. https://www.privateinternetaccess. com/blog/2017/05/coming-another-call-everyones-dna-collected-stored-permanently/. Licensed under CC BY-SA 4.0 International.

As you read, consider the following questions:

1. Why did Sir Alec Jeffreys say that a DNA catalog would be the fairest system?
2. How much does a DNA sequencing cost today?
3. Why won't law enforcement need to store tissue and fingerprint samples in the future?

The head of the Hamburg Institute for Legal Medicine, Klaus Püschel, has called for the DNA of everybody in Germany—including tourists—to be collected and stored. As a story in the German news magazine *Der Spiegel* reported, Püschel wants this because:

> "Then we can clear up crimes much faster and much better, because we can tell from whom every clue at a crime scene comes."

This isn't the first time that such a call has been made. Back in 2002, the inventor of DNA fingerprinting, Professor Sir Alec Jeffreys, said that collecting and storing everyone's DNA would be the fairest system:

> "If we're all on the database, we're all in exactly the same boat—the issue of discrimination disappears."

Jeffreys was concerned about the fact that the genetic fingerprints—special regions of the DNA that can be used to identify people with a high degree of accuracy—of those suspected of crimes but later cleared were still being stored by the UK authorities. He believed this was discriminatory.

His idea of creating a DNA database for the entire population was not taken up, and the retention of the DNA profiles for millions of innocent citizens remained a serious problem in the UK. The battle to end the practice was taken to the European Court of Human Rights (ECHR), where the UK government lost. The ECHR judges ruled that keeping the DNA fingerprints of two innocent men "could not be regarded as necessary in a democratic society." As a result, the UK brought in new rules that enable those not convicted of crimes to have their DNA fingerprints deleted. But the UK's DNA database remains relatively large. In 2016, there were nearly 6 million records held—almost a tenth of the UK population. For comparison, the National DNA Index in the US has around 15 million DNA profiles—about 5% of the national population.

The proposal to create a DNA database of the complete German population is unlikely to come to fruition because of the country's long-standing concerns about privacy. More concrete plans in Kuwait have already been watered-down for the same reason. Last year, Kuwait announced that it intended to collect the DNA of everyone in the country—including visitors—but this idea has now been scaled back.

The Kuwaiti authorities have not released any details of what precautions they will be taking to hold the DNA fingerprints safely, but Püschel has laid out his suggestions. Der Spiegel reports:

> "According to the lawyer, the data should be stored in a completely safe place, 'deep down in a mine', and also completely protected against hacker attacks. Several judges should watch over access to the data, which are only to be disclosed in clearly defined cases, such as abduction, rape, murder and homicide."

Hamburg's data protection commissioner, Johannes Caspar, is not impressed. Despite the precautions Püschel would want to see, Caspar says that storing the genetic data of everyone is neither compatible with the presumption of innocence nor with the principle of proportionality. But Püschel insists the DNA fingerprint is "just a number":

> "There is nothing about our personality, no one knows what eye color you have or whether you have gray hair, they're just like lottery numbers."

He's right: DNA fingerprints are just like hash codes – a unique but meaningless distillation of a much larger data set. That makes them easy to obtain—you only need to look at certain regions of DNA—and very cheap to store as digital data. But soon it will be feasible to sequence the entire human genome, not just the fingerprint, and to store the gigabyte or so of digital data that results (the human genome has around three billion chemical "letters," using a quaternary rather than binary encoding system.)

The total cost of obtaining the first nearly-complete sequence of human DNA was around $750 million. Since then, sequencing costs have been falling dramatically—faster than Moore's Law. Today, a person's DNA can be sequenced for around $1000, and companies say they can get that down to $100 soon. It won't be long before a full read-out of your DNA costs less then a simple blood test, and can be carried out using a portable device smaller than a smartphone.

Once that happens, the police will no longer need to keep tissue samples taken from people, along with the DNA fingerprint: they will simply sequence the entire DNA, which will be more accurate, and allow for matches in cases where the DNA found on a crime scene is partial or degraded. There will be pressure to do that because it will be much cheaper and safer to store petabytes of DNA data than to preserve millions of bulky and perishable physical samples.

Similarly, it will also become possible to sequence and store everyone's DNA as part of their medical records. That would give doctors important insights into every person's genetic and thus physical make-up. The benefits are clear. But as Rick Falkvinge noted last year, if genetic information has been obtained for medical purposes, the temptation to use it for solving crimes is almost irresistible for the authorities.

Once this happened, Püschel's dream of a complete DNA database that could be used to solve crimes would be realized, but without the safeguards he recommends. It would not simply be the meaningless hash of DNA data, but the complete data set. That would not only reveal your eye color, and whether you have gray hair, but also some predispositions to medical conditions you might have. That could be deeply problematic. For example, imagine if opponents could point to genetic traits associated with a likelihood of physical or mental health problems in the DNA of top politicians or CEOs of major companies. Similarly, possessing the genetic code of everyone would also allow them to be cross-referenced to prove—or disprove—paternity and maternity. Discovering hitherto secret biological relationships in this way might make some people open to blackmail, or lead to marital breakdowns and suicides.

Another troubling possibility is that evidence could be faked. If somebody's DNA sequence were available, it would be straightforward to synthesize strands of it, and then to plant them at the scene of a crime to be found by forensic teams. Because DNA matching is so precise, it would be very hard to convince the courts that the person concerned had not been physically present.

Finally, there are even more futuristic and sinister possibilities if full DNA sequences can be analyzed. For example, it would be possible to create genetically targeted bio-weapons that only work against the DNA of one person in particular, while leaving everyone else unharmed. To investigators, the illness or death of one person would simply seem to be due to an unknown factor, or just chance. The same technique could also be deployed for high-tech genocide by creating biological weapons that only affect a particular ethnic group sharing common genetic traits.

The central problem here is not the sequencing of people's DNA, which is certain to become more common as costs plummet, but the creation of centralized stores of genetic data, for example by the police or as part of the medical system. As we know, there is no such thing as a secure database—even if it is airgapped, bribery and corruption of those with authorized access to it will always make it vulnerable. It may not be possible, or even desirable, to stop everyone's complete genome being sequenced, but we must ensure that it is only ever stored in a distributed form that limits the harm when the most personal digital data of all—DNA—starts to leak, as it inevitably will.

"There are still many bio-ethical considerations to think through. The biggest point of debate is informed consent."

Openly Sharing Genetic Data Creates Active Participation in Scientific Research

Bastian Greshake

In the following viewpoint, Bastian Greshake argues that some people have chosen to share their DNA through the internet, even through their own websites, making them active participants in medical research. Several projects, including the Personal Genome Project, offer platforms for consumers who want to share. But this "openness" may come at a cost. Bastian Greshake holds a PhD in Bioinformatics from Goethe University in Frankurt am Main, Germany, and is director of research for Open Humans Foundation. He founded an open data repository that allows people to donate their DNA samples to the public domain.

As you read, consider the following questions:

1. What is the oldest project to which consumers can openly share their genetic information?
2. According to this viewpoint, what is the main argument against open-sharing of DNA information?
3. Why are pseudonyms not effective as a way to de-identify DNA data?

The price of gene sequencing has plummeted in the last few decades. Now we can know what our DNA looks like, and discover what our bodies may have in store for us in the future. We can know medical information such as how long asthma will last to our likelihood of getting certain types of cancer.

23andMe is the largest genetic testing company, providing DNA analysis directly to over 200,000 customers worldwide. Its test is not meant to be a diagnostic tool, but is intended for research and educational purposes. It detects about a million genetic markers from the human genome. These markers are associated with a range of traits from bitter taste perception or eye colour to vulnerability to diseases such as Parkinson's or Alzheimer's.

Genome-Wide Association Studies are used to establish the link between markers and traits. Such studies are conducted by comparing the genetic makers in a sample of people who have a specific trait to a control population who don't. To give reliable results, a study needs to have a sufficiently large number of participants, with thousands or better ten thousands of people enrolled. This can be an obstacle, but 23andMe has realised the potential of its large customer base, and uses the data of consenting clients in its research.

A US Supreme Court ruling on gene patents last month means that tests on naturally-occuring genes such as BRCA1 and BRCA2 can no longer be monopolised by private companies, though synthetic DNA can still be patented. This represents a significant hurdle cleared for genetic testing, with lower costs giving

Anonymous DNA Samples Can Still Reveal Individual Identity

One MIT researcher identified individuals and their extended families by using only anonymous DNA samples and public records of people's ages and addresses. Someone's DNA sample can reveal information that she might not want publicly revealed.

For instance, 23andMe says its tests can clue people in to whether they have a genetic variation that could increase their risk of developing a health condition or whether they're carriers for certain diseases. Furthermore, its privacy policy warns that it will store and process your information in countries that "may have laws that are different from those of your country of residence." In other words, less protective laws.

Very few consumers know these risks. And the lengthy terms of service, privacy and consent documents are not only difficult to understand, they are difficult to coalesce into a simple understanding of the various risks.

"DNA Testing: Americans Sign Away Their Rights," by Twila Brase, StarTribune, April 6, 2018.

more people the chance to get tested, hence providing more data for studies. But sharing the data of people involved in research is a delicate subject.

Sharing data isn't a big part of our culture. Privacy is a large issue for genetic testing. What happens if employers, insurance companies or the government get access to the data? Can they use it to fire you, raise your insurance rates or as evidence in criminal investigations?

The law can protect individuals to some extent. For instance, in the US, the Genetic Information Non-Discrimination Act is designed to prevent the use of genetic information in employment and health insurance. But they may not offer protection from all negative uses of genetic information. The US laws do not cover long-term care or life insurance.

Despite these issues, many individuals who purchased personal genetic test results have published them openly on the internet—often on their own websites—to give the world access to their data. This also has the benefit of changing their role from passive research subject to active agent of scientific endeavour. The first projects, which try to offer a platform for people who want to share their genetic data with the world, have already started.

One of the oldest is the Personal Genome Project, which started in 2006 at the Harvard Medical School. Volunteers can enroll in the study, which aims to publish the full genomes along with medical records of 100,000 participants into the public domain.

Another such project is openSNP, which we started in 2011. It allows genetic testing customers to publish their data, along with traits they have, into the public domain. OpenSNP also mines the scientific literature for the different genetic markers tested by companies like 23andMe and acts as a platform where people can discuss genetic variants, recent studies and test results.

Although neither project has the number of users to allow large scale studies, the data is already being put to use. Last year, the Personal Genomics Project (PGP) started the GET-Evidence database, a tool for the automatic annotation of genetic variations. And data from openSNP is already being used by the genetic genealogy community to compare old DNA samples like that of Ötzi the Iceman or the ancient Denisovan. Individual openSNP users are also testing their own annotation software with the available data and returning the results.

But this openness may come at a cost, and there are still many bio-ethical considerations to think through. The biggest point of debate is informed consent. It is arguable whether participants of projects such as the PGP or openSNP have understood the potential risks they take by making their data available. While users can participate in both projects with a pseudonym, it will always be possible to identify them because of the unique nature of an individual's genome.

To tackle this worry, the PGP limits its participants to permanent residents of the US and each one has to take a series of online tests. This meets the standards of the Institutional Review Board (IRB) of Harvard Medical School. OpenSNP has no such process, as it is run outside of the academic sphere with no funding, making it more difficult to get IRB approval.

But even without projects such as the PGP or openSNP, people would not stop sharing their genetic data via websites, source code-platforms like GitHub or even Facebook. Right now, technical progress is moving too fast for legislation and bioethical best practices to catch up. Propositions like Portable Legal Consent are taking the first steps to adapt human subject research for a culture of sharing in the internet age. But we have a long way to go before we can enjoy all the benefits that collaborating and openly sharing data can bring to human genetics.

> *"We should not be using HeLa cells because no consent was obtained to take them. And I am very uncomfortable with the general idea that heirs/descendants should be allowed to retroactively consent for a dead relative. Nothing that can happen now or in the future can make up for the lack of real consent."*

A Family's Right to Genetic Privacy Does Not Trump an Individual's Right to Publish Their Genome

Michael Eisen

In the following viewpoint Michael Eisen argues that individuals have the right to publish their genetic information, even though that could impact the privacy and rights of their relatives and descendants. Eisen uses the case of Henrietta Lacks, an African-American woman whose cells were obtained and used for research without her consent. The author believes there is no question about the importance of individual consent, but that does not extend to familial privacy. Michael Eisen is a biologist at UC Berkeley and an Investigator of the Howard Hughes Medical Institute.

As you read, consider the following questions:

1. What are HeLa cells?
2. Why does the author disagree with Rebecca Skloot's *New York Times* piece?
3. Why does the author compare Lacks to Jim Watson or Craig Venter?

Rebecca Skloot has an essay in today's *New York Times* discussing the recent publication of the genome sequence of a widely used human cell line. Skloot, as most of you already know, wrote a book about the history of this cell line—known as HeLa for Henrietta Lacks, the woman from whom they were obtained.

In her book, Skloot describes how the cells were taken from Lacks, who was dying of aggressive ovarian cancer, without her knowledge or consent, and how the family was kept in the dark about the cells for decades, even as they researchers showed up to take samples from Lacks' descendants. Skloot has done a wonderful job of not only gaining the Lacks family's support for her book, but of engaging them with the legacy of Henrietta's unwitting contribution to science and medicine.

So it makes sense that Skloot would take umbrage with the release of the complete sequence of HeLa cells, published without the consent of knowledge of the Lacks family. I can understand how this happened—HeLa cells are so ubiquitous in the lab, it's easy to forget that they come from a real person (although it's hard to believe the authors of the paper hadn't read, or at least heard of, Skloot's book). But it's really not acceptable, something the authors now realize and are trying to correct.

Unfortunately, Skloot's NYT essay on this topic was muddled—conflating two distinct issues—one very general, the other specific to HeLa cells—that have to be dealt with separately.

The first issue is one of consent from Henrietta Lacks to sequence and publish the genome of cells derived from her body. As Skloot made very clear in her book, no such consent was obtained.

And, since Lacks died a long time ago, it can not be obtained. Lots of people, including Skloot, point out that consent was neither required nor generally obtained in the 1950's when Lacks was sick. And knowing that Lacks was a poor African-American woman, it's hard not to see more sinister overtones in her treatment.

To me, there really is no moral question here. We should not be using HeLa cells because no consent was obtained to take them. And I am very uncomfortable with the general idea that heirs/descendants should be allowed to retroactively consent for a dead relative. Nothing that can happen now or in the future can make up for the lack of real consent. But whether they should be used or not, these cells are being used all over the planet. Given that this is unlikely to change, there's really no choice but to de facto give the Lacks family a kind of proxy consenting power to act on Henrietta's behalf.

However Skloot's piece glides from the issue of how to retroactively get Henrietta's permission to experiment with and publish about her cells to the seemingly related issue of whether publication of the HeLa cell genome is an invasion of the privacy of Lacks' living relatives. Skloot repeatedly raises the issue of all the things we can learn about an individual and their relatives by sequencing their DNA, and whether family members should have some kind of veto power over the publishing of a relative's genome.

But this is very different than the question of how to obtain consent from an individual who is no longer alive. To see why, let's stipulate that Henrietta Lacks had consented to all these studies— had, in sound mind, given permission for the doctors to take her cell lines, establish cultures, send them around the world to be used for any purpose and to freely publish the results of any studies on these cells. Would you still require the authors of the paper to consent Lacks' family?

Skloot clearly thinks the answer is yes—positing that publishing any individual's genome sequence is intrinsically an invasion of the privacy of their relatives—whether or not the sequenced individual consented to the process. Hence this quote:

"That is private family information," said Jeri Lacks-Whye, Lacks's granddaughter. "It shouldn't have been published without our consent."

This has nothing to do with the history of Henrietta Lacks and HeLa cells. It is an active assertion about familial privacy rights that would—if you accept it—be just as true if the paper in question had described the sequencing of anyone else's genome. Why weren't the same issues raised when the genome belonged not to Henrietta Lacks, but to Jim Watson or Craig Venter?

I find the way Skloot's NYT piece moves back and forth between the historical transgressions against Henrietta Lacks and the contemporary threat to her relatives' privacy incredibly misleading. I doubt this was intentional—rather I think it reflects muddled thinking on her part about these issues. But either way, by juxtaposing the entirely justifiable empowering of the Lacks family to grant individual consent on Henrietta's behalf with the desire of the same family to protect its genetic privacy, Skloot is implying that these are one and the same—that we should give ANY family the right to veto the publication of a relative's genome.

But this is a logical fallacy. We probably all agree that the Lacks family should have been consulted about the publication of the HeLa genome because Henrietta herself never gave such permission. And some of you (not me) may think that a family's right to genetic privacy trumps the right of an individual to publish their genome. But the former does not, in any way, imply the latter, and I think Skloot did the conversation around these issues a huge disservice by conflating them in such a prominent way.

> "With a second DNA sample, an individual's genetic information could be pulled out of what was thought to be anonymous 'pooled' genomic data or gene activity databases."

Researchers Can Identify Anonymous Genetic Information

Susan Young Rojahn

In the following viewpoint, Susan Young Rojahn argues that scientific researchers can still identify contributors of DNA even when the samples are anonymized. They could achieve this through publicly available information on the internet just as legal investigators might do. Rojahn calls for improved and comprehensive legal protection of genetic information and better education for scientific study participants so they are aware of the privacy risks. Susan Young Rojahn is the biomedicine editor at MIT Technology Review. She holds a PhD from the University of Texas Medical Branch at Galveston.

"Study Highlights the Risk of Handing Over Your Genome," by Susan Young Rojahn, MIT Technology Review, January 17, 2013. Reprinted by permission.

As you read, consider the following questions:

1. What is the stance of the Council for Responsible Genetics?
2. How many people did researchers at the Whitehead Institute for Biomedical Research identify in public genomic data sets?
3. What methods did this team of researchers use to deanonymize genetic data?

If you contribute your genome sequence anonymously to a scientific study, that data might still be linked back to you, according to a study published today in the journal *Science*. The researchers behind the study found they could deanonymize genomic data using only publicly available Internet information and some clever detective work.

The study points to rising issues concerning genetic privacy and the need for better legal protection against genetic discrimination, experts say, since such a technique could reveal a person's propensity to a particular disease. The work also shows that study participants need to be better educated about the risks of joining genetic research efforts.

Open-access data sets of human genomic information are an important resource for researchers trying to uncover the genetic basis of human disease. The 1000 Genomes Project, for example, is a publicly available catalog of variation in humans that researchers can use to identify mutations that cause disease risk in certain populations. Researchers use this kind of open database much more often than controlled access sources, the National Institutes of Health said in a response to today's findings that was also published in *Science*.

"Our last intention is to push these resources behind some firewall, says Yaniv Erlich, a geneticist at the Whitehead Institute for Biomedical Research and senior author on today's study. "We are in favor of public data sharing, but we need to think about how it could be misused and describe that correctly to people."

While the Genetic Information Nondiscrimination Act of 2008 offers people some protection against employers or health insurers discriminating against them based on their genetics, life insurers and disability insurers are not prevented from using such information in their decisions.

"We have no comprehensive genetic privacy law," says Jeremy Gruber, a lawyer and president of the Council for Responsible Genetics. "People need to be much better informed of the lack of privacy protections we have for genetic information," says Gruber.

In the long run, says Erlich, it is better for these potential breaches to be demonstrated by a friendly investigator rather than someone who really wants to exploit the data. "That would really undermine the public trust," he says.

This isn't the first time privacy risks have been highlighted for public genome databases. Different groups have shown that with a second DNA sample, an individual's genetic information could be pulled out of what was thought to be anonymous "pooled" genomic data or gene activity databases. But Erlich's team used only knowledge of genetic markers and Internet detective work to identify nearly 50 people in public genomic data sets.

Erlich, a former computer security researcher, was once hired by banks and other businesses to test their computer systems. For the DNA sleuthing, Erlich and his team used free genealogical databases that link surnames with genetic markers, called short tandem repeats, on the Y chromosome. There is no known biological function for these repeats, but the length and number are commonly used in ancestry research because, like surnames, those patterns are typically passed from father to son.

Once the team found a link between the Y chromosome repeats in the genomic databases and potential surnames, they used other pieces of demographic information, such as date and place of birth, which are included in some of the genomic databases, and public records to identify donors.

Eric Green, director of the National Human Genome Research Institute, and other employees of the NIH acknowledge that Erlich's study highlights vulnerabilities in these research projects. To mitigate future risks, they write in the response published in Science, the NIH has decided to "shift age information, which had been available for some of the participants on the repository's public Web site, into controlled-access portions of the resource."

In addition to recruiting people who think the societal and medical research benefits of participating in genomic research outweigh the risks, better legal protection is key, says George Church, a geneticist at Harvard Medical School and founder of the Personal Genome Project, an open-access database of genomic and health data. While there may be ways to make the data more secure, "for every lock there is going to be a countermeasure, and I think that's a game that's just not worth playing," says Church. "Much better is coming up with a protocol where you don't need any locks," he says, which would include better legal protection and education for study participants.

Today's findings emphasize the need for public representation in the oversight of data collection, says Wylie Burke, a clinical geneticist at the University of Washington in Seattle. "Information should be readily available to the public concerning the oversight procedures in place, the research purposes for which data are being used, the outcomes of data uses, and, of course, how any misuses of data have been handled," she says. "Without this kind of approach, we could see increasing mistrust of the research process."

> "*The business model for the ancestry testing industry is also unique, reflecting the unequal power relationship between the consumer and the testing companies.*"

Direct-to-Consumer DNA Testing Kits Use a New Business Model for Testing Company Advantage

Sheldon Krimsky and David Cay Johnston

In the following excerpted viewpoint, Sheldon Krimsky and David Kay Johnston argue in their analysis of AncestryDNA's testing service agreements, consumers must be aware of the potential privacy risks. They claim testing companies overpromise and under-deliver on those promises. Sheldon Krimsky is Lenore Stern Professor of Humanities and Social Sciences and adjunct professor in public health and community medicine at Tufts University. His research focuses on the linkages between science and technology, ethics, and public policy. David Cay Johnston is an investigative reporter and columnist. He has been a distinguished visiting lecturer at Syracuse University College of Law and Whitman School of Management.

"Ancestry DNA Testing and Privacy: A Consumer Guide," by Sheldon Krimsky and David Cay Johnston, Council for Responsible Genetics, March 2017. Reprinted by permission.

As you read, consider the following questions:

1. According to this viewpoint, what are the privacy issues with consumer DNA testing?
2. How many companies offered direct-to-consumer DNA testing in 2015?
3. In the study referenced, what percentage of companies permitted disclosure to third parties?

Since direct to consumer genetic tests were first introduced, privacy concerns have been raised. Ancestry clients send their swabbed cells as well as personal data to a company. Their DNA sequences are kept on file along with personal data.[17] Among the privacy issues are: who gets access to the DNA and personal information?; is the DNA sample kept after the DNA is sequenced?; can the company sell the information?; can the criminal justice system access the information?; what third parties can be affected if the information becomes available to others?; does the company have a research arm that would place the private information into a research database?; can information that has been anonymized be de-identified and what protections do consumers have against this?

Wallace et al. (2015) noted: "Given expertise, resources and will, it is possible to re-identify individuals from anonymized family history data suggesting that procedures such as name removal and encoding are not sufficient to protect against privacy breaches."[18] For example, in cases where a researcher knows the family tree information associated with an "anonymized" record, the record can be de-anonymized. There is also evidence that consumers do not pay much attention to privacy issues and sign consent forms without carefully reading them or understanding the warrants and liabilities.[19]

A study examined the privacy policies of 228 direct-to-consumer genetics testing companies in 2015, including companies offering medical genetics, paternity and ancestry DNA tests. The study concluded: "DTCGT [direct-to-consumer genetic tests]

Legal Pressure Pushes Testing Companies to Share Privacy Policy Details

Pressure is growing on direct-to-consumer genealogy and genetic testing companies to be more transparent about their privacy policies, after the arrest of the notorious Golden State Killer using publicly available data from one of the websites.

In a letter sent this week—and shared with STAT—Reps. Dave Loebsack of Iowa and Frank Pallone Jr. of New Jersey peppered four of the platforms with questions about their security systems and customer privacy. The Democratic lawmakers are hoping to work with the companies—23andMe, AncestryDNA, Family Tree DNA, and National Geographic Geno—to identify and resolve any privacy and security issues. And they're in a prime position to do so: They sit on the Energy and Commerce committee, which handles both health care and privacy issues in technology.

"Much more often than not, Congress acts after the horse is out of the barn," Loebsack said. "I want to try to partner with genetic testing services to address any potential challenges before there are actually breaches of trust."

"Lawmakers Press Genetic Testing Companies for Details on Their Privacy Policies," by Megan Thielking, STAT, June 21, 2018.

companies either have separate privacy policies or include their privacy policy in their contract. Many DTCGT companies' privacy policies focus more on data that may be collected on a website via the use of cookies, rather than what is done with genetic data specifically."[20] The study found: 48% of the companies allow for disclosure of personal data or genetic data to third parties in certain circumstances; 25% state that they may disclose data to law enforcement agencies, to comply with the law, courts or health agencies; only 10% will destroy the physical sample either immediately after sequencing or after communicating test results.

The Business of DNA Ancestry Testing

Companies selling DNA ancestry testing make it seem like fun, distracting customers from how such tests pose grave threats to consumer privacy that can disrupt families, cause emotional distress, and even affect financial wellbeing. The genetic industry relies on a new business model largely untested in legislatures and courts of law. Basically, customers pay companies to acquire onto information from which the companies, but not their customers, can profit directly. Historically companies paid for such information, they did not collect payment from those providing it.

Consumers who pay for such tests lose control over their most intimate personal information, the genetic material that makes each person unique. Consumers also relinquish valuable economic rights. The testing companies, and those to which they license, prohibit consumers who paid for genetic tests from sharing in profits from medical products and services based on their genetic information (discussed further below).[21]

Genetic tests that promise to tell people about their ancestors are rapidly gaining in popularity, spurred by ubiquitous advertising that promises to reliably answer who you are. Ancestry DNA companies identify specific information from your genes, the thousands of components in each of your 46 chromosomes that form the basic unit of inheritance determining your unique characteristics as well as parts of your DNA that do not make up your genes (noncoding inter-genic regions). You inherited half of your chromosomes from each parent, as did your parents and so on back through time.

Engaging television ads promise to reveal who your ancestors were, sometimes in ways that undo family lore. In one commercial a cheerful man who grew up being told his ancestors were German discovers that they were Scottish, and so he trades the family lederhosen for kilts. Other ads promise to reveal your ancestral history with a precision that is scientifically impossible. One radio commercial touts a young man's delight at discovering that he is 18 percent Viking—ignoring the fact that no genetic test can tell if one's ancestors were explorers, traders, and pirates or did any other kind of work. While that commercial can be understood as taking literary license in describing Nordic ancestry, it also illustrates how companies engaged in scientific pursuit will twist facts to further their commercial interests. There is even a broadcast commercial asserting that DNA analysis will reveal a propensity for sleeping on your back rather than your side or stomach.

These and other commercial pitches make genetics, the science of inherited traits, seem like modern magic. And it's easy magic. Just pay $99 or more for a test kit, swab the inside of your mouth, and mail in the cotton tip to get a supposedly complete report on where your ancestors came from—and perhaps much more.

Consumers should be extremely wary as these come-ons promise more than they can deliver, ignoring problems with accuracy while obscuring a business model in which customers pay for the privilege of giving away valuable information to venture capitalists who expect it will make them very, very rich. "The long game here is not to make money selling kits, although the kits are essential to get the base level," said Patrick Chung, a 23andMe board member and partner in New Enterprise Associates, a global venture capital firm. "Once you have the data [the company] does actually become the Google of personalized healthcare."[22]

[...]

The business model for the ancestry testing industry is also unique, reflecting the unequal power relationship between the consumer and the testing companies. Consumers pay for the tests, but simultaneously give away rights to their personal genetic information. Ancestry DNA companies are then free to use the genetic material of many people to develop medical tests, products, services and treatments. The DNA testing companies and the manufacturers to which they license data will get all the profits from such products. Consumers will get nothing because they give away their property rights over their own genetic information. Venture capitalists serve on the boards of ancestry companies, expecting huge future profits from using the information that consumers paid the ancestry DNA companies to test.

There are few privacy protections in the contracts consumers must sign to get their genetic material tested, and what little protection these contracts provide can be voided. Your credit card agreement contains more safeguards than the contracts offered by ancestry DNA companies, which are long on benefits for the companies and nearly devoid of meaningful protections for customers. These consumers effectively relinquish control of their genetic material even if they remove it from the database of the testing firm, or firms, they paid to analyze their genetic material. No government regulatory agency audits to protect against surreptitious use of the data. Many contracts even allow companies to change their terms and conditions at will without notifying each customer in advance.

[...]

Notes

17. Ancestry.com maintains: "Our service providers act on 23andMe's behalf. While we implement procedures and contractual terms to protect the confidentiality and security of your information, we cannot guarantee the confidentiality and security of your information due to the inherent risks associated with storing and transmitting data electronically....We may share aggregate information with third-parties, which is any information that has been stripped of your Registration Information (e.g., your name and contact information) and aggregated with information of others so that you cannot reasonably be identified as an individual ("Aggregate Information")." The operative term here is "you cannot reasonably be identified." https://www.23andMe.com/en-gb/about/privacy. Accessed March 3, 2017.

18. Susan E. Wallace, Eli G. Gourna, Viktoriya Niolova and Nucola A. Sheehan. "Family tree and ancestry inference: is there a need for 'generational' consent." *BMC Medical Ethics* 16:87–96 (2015), p. 94.

19. Wallace et al. 2015, p. 94.

20. Andelka M. Phillips. "Genetic privacy and direct-to-consumer genetics." IEEE CS Security and Privacy Workshops. 2015, pp. 60–64 at p. 62.

21. The company Portable Genomics, which deals with health information, advertises that consumers may realize financial benefits from contributing their DNA and health information.

22. Elizabeth Murphy, "Inside 23andMe Founder Ann Wojcicki's $99 DNA Revolution." *Fast Company*, October 13, 2014. https://www.fastcompany.com/3018598/for-99-this-ceo-can-tell-you-what-might-kill-you-inside-23andme-founder-anne-wojcickis-dna-r. Accessed January 25, 2017.

> "We must ensure we provide good information about genetic testing to everyone. But we can, and should, explore different ways of delivering that information. In fact we must actively, creatively and energetically explore this. Because it will not be possible to deliver genetic medicine at scale, if upfront one-on-one discussions with a genetic counsellor are needed for every test."

Integrate Direct-to-Consumer Testing into Genetic Medicine

Nazneen Rahman

In the following viewpoint Nazneen Rahman argues that DTC genetic testing is becoming more affordable and available, and the genetic medicine community should embrace it. The author examines the BRCA testing offered by companies such as 23andMe, noting that testing is not as comprehensive as it could be. Also, the author notes that consumers often don't know how to interpret or emotionally process their online test results and that testing companies and genetics professionals should come together to integrate their services in the future. Nazneen Rahman is program director at the Transforming Genetic Medicine Initiative.

As you read, consider the following questions:

1. How many BRCA mutations are tested in 23andMe's DTC tests?
2. Why are some newer BRCA tests less complete than older ones?
3. How could those with positive tests be guided according to the viewpoint?

There has been a flurry of articles this week on the FDA's decision to allow 23andMe to sell direct-to-consumer (DTC) tests for three mutations in the BRCA cancer predisposition genes. Anyone can buy the test, over the internet, without involvement of a health professional.

Direct-to-consumer companies say they are empowering people and democratizing access to genetic testing. But many people are worried. Particularly genetic counsellors. Can you be adequately informed about BRCA testing online? Should a test for only three BRCA mutations be sold? Will people be falsely reassured about their cancer risk if their 23andMe BRCA test is negative?

How worried should we be about direct-to-consumer genetic testing? Are we worrying about the right things? Are the concerns really only about direct-to-consumer testing, or do they also apply to conventional testing?

We Must Provide Good Information about Genetic Testing

It is the responsibility of a genetic test provider to make sure anyone thinking about taking a test has clear information to guide their decision. Genetic counselling is often stated to be the "gold standard" way to do this. But the reality is more diverse, because people and their situations are diverse.

Many people find the personal one-to-one discussion with a genetic counsellor invaluable. But there are also many people who find it difficult and frustrating to have to wait for an appointment, to take time off work, to travel to and from the clinic. Particularly if they have researched testing, and have already come to an informed decision.

We must ensure we provide good information about genetic testing to everyone. But we can, and should, explore different ways of delivering that information. In fact we must actively, creatively and energetically explore this. Because it will not be possible to deliver genetic medicine at scale, if upfront one-on-one discussions with a genetic counsellor are needed for every test.

We Should Embrace New Ways of Communicating Information

People are variable and changeable in how they like to consume information. Many of us have changed dramatically about this over the last few years. We are now choosing online ways to do things that we used to want to do face-to-face with experts.

Of course, making a decision about your health is different from planning a holiday. But this doesn't necessarily mean it's fine to order a holiday online but not a genetic test. It just means we have to be extra careful that the online processes for ordering genetic tests are appropriate, safe and well-regulated.

Direct-to-Consumer and Genetic Counsellor Communications Are Pretty Similar

There are more similarities between the direct-to-consumer and genetic counsellor models of testing than people realise. Genetic clinics have standard genetic testing information sheets that they give to everyone. Many have online written and video information as well. In concept and content, these are very similar to the videos and online materials that direct-to-consumer companies use.

This carefully prepared, consistent information is very important. It should be the foundation of all genetic testing communications. People can go back to the information whenever they need to refresh their understanding. And it provides a vital safety-net if you accidentally forget to say something in the consultation.

Some online genetic test providers have genetic counsellors that you can speak with, if you have extra questions. Others, like 23andMe, do not offer this. But they do recommend speaking to a genetic counsellor, prior to buying a test, if you have unanswered questions (though it is in small print!).

So, there is consensus that anyone having a genetic test should have clear, comprehensive, written and/or visual information about it. There is also consensus that people who have unanswered questions should be directed to someone who can help them. The two key things we need to decide are 1) how do we make sure people recognise they need extra information, and then get that information. 2) which tests should only be ordered if you have spoken with a genetic counsellor as well as reading the standard information.

Many BRCA Tests Only Look at a Few Mutations

Another worry people have voiced about the 23andMe BRCA test, is that it only looks at three mutations that are found in people of Ashkenazi heritage. There are only about 300,000 Ashkenazim in the UK, and about 10 million in the US. So the test isn't very useful to most people. But many BRCA tests ordered through genetic clinics also only test for a limited set of mutations. Historically, one of the main roles of genetic counsellors was to work out which mutations a person should be tested for.

This made sense when gene tests were expensive. The cost of an Ashkenazi BRCA test used to be one tenth of the cost of a complete BRCA test. Now the costs are equivalent and it doesn't make sense to do a limited test. There will always be people that have mutations not tested for, however carefully one tries to work out which is the likely mutation. And one of the basic advantages of fast, cheap DNA testing is that we can stop the guessing and just do the testing.

We stopped doing limited BRCA testing three years ago and we do full BRCA testing on anyone that was previously eligible for the limited tests. All testing providers should aim to provide comprehensive BRCA tests as soon as possible.

Some Newer BRCA Tests Are Less Complete than Older Ones

There is another problem with the completeness of BRCA tests that is not well appreciated and not well signposted by BRCA test providers. An important type of disease-causing mutation in the BRCA genes is tricky to detect with new sequencing methods, even whole genome sequencing. We wrote about these tricky exon CNVs in previous blogs. Some BRCA test providers have solved the problem using deep sequencing and clever informatics, some by using a separate test to detect exon CNVs, but some simply don't test for them. This is a problem. Exon CNVs account for 1 in 10 BRCA mutations, including one of the commonest BRCA mutations in the UK.

Most people, including genetic specialists, assume the BRCA test they've ordered is fully comprehensive, because the traditional BRCA tests had to cover exon CNVs. Even if you are aware of the issue it can be very difficult to find out how good the test you've ordered is at detecting exon CNVs.

So incomplete testing is a general issue for the BRCA genes. And transparency about the extent and quality of genetic testing is a general problem for genetic medicine. It needs urgent attention.

False Reassurance Is a General Problem

Another common concern about the 23andMe BRCA test is that people with a negative test will be falsely reassured that they don't have a BRCA mutation at all. This is a real issue, and some people will believe they are free of BRCA mutations if their 23andMe test is negative. Those voicing this concern say this would not happen if the person had genetic counselling. That has not been our experience.

Over the years, many people attending our clinics have told us they don't have a BRCA mutation. Then we see their test report and find they were only tested for the three Ashkenazi mutations. Usually their report is very clear about this. Usually a genetic counsellor has also talked to them and written to them clearly about it. Nevertheless, the person has come to believe that they were negative for all BRCA mutations, not just three mutations.

All communications are susceptible to this type of misunderstanding. However, clearly when we say something, there is a chance that people will hear something else! The best way to reduce this particular false assumption is to make fully comprehensive BRCA testing the standard. Then the assumption will be correct.

We Need to Focus on People Who Have Positive Tests

Many of the concerns about the 23andMe BRCA test have focused on people with negative tests. But I find myself more concerned about the people who find out they have a BRCA mutation through direct-to-consumer testing. I have been involved in some instances over the last few years because the 23andMe BRCA test was not banned in the UK. Although 23andMe clearly state that anyone with a positive test should seek confirmation and advice from a health professional, they do not guide people on how to do this. And they do not take any responsibility for ensuring that it happens. This leaves people anxious and guideless. And it leaves health systems with the task of handling the emotional, logistical and financial fall-out.

We need to decide how people who discover they have BRCA mutations through direct-to-consumer testing will be managed. I don't think it is reasonable for the direct-to-consumer companies to abrogate all responsibility. At the very least they should contribute to the NHS, perhaps through an annual license-to-operate fee, to cover the cost of integrating these individuals back into NHS care.

We Should Integrate Direct-to-Consumer Testing into Genetic Medicine

It would be good to move on from the "direct-to-consumer is bad and genetic counselling is good" assumption that has underpinned most of the dialogue on this topic in recent years. Instead we should think about how we can best serve the needs and choices of people considering genetic testing. There may well be situations where direct-to-consumer tests have a useful role to play. We need to make the most of these opportunities.

Most importantly, genetic medicine must retain control of the regulation and integration of genetic testing in healthcare, however it is provided.

Periodical and Internet Sources Bibliography

The following articles have been selected to supplement the diverse views presented in this chapter.

Erin Brodwin, "DNA-Testing Company 23andMe Has Signed a $300 Million Deal with a Drug Giant. Here's How to Delete Your Data If That Freaks You Out," *Business Insider*, July 25, 2018. www.businessinsider.com/dna-testing-delete-your-data-23andme-ancestry-2018-7.

Roberta Estes, "Beware the Sale of Your DNA—Just Because You Can Upload Doesn't Mean You Should," DNAeXplained—Genetic Genealogy, May 25, 2016. https://dna-explained.com/2016/05/25/beware-the-sale-of-your-dna-just-because-you-can-upload-doesnt-mean-you-should/.

Caitlin Fairchild, "23andMe and Other Genetic Testing Companies Release Guideline on How to Handle DNA Data," Nextgov, August 2, 2018. www.nextgov.com/analytics-data/2018/08/23andme-and-other-genetic-testing-companies-release-guideline-how-handle-dna-data/150243/.

Finjan Cybersecurity, "Home DNA Tests Could Be Gathering Your Personal Info! A Discussion of Genetic Testing Privacy Issues," December 26, 2017. https://blog.finjan.com/genetic-testing-privacy/.

Laura Geggel, "23andMe Is Sharing Genetic Data with Drug Giant," *Scientific American*, July 28, 2018. www.scientificamerican.com/article/23andme-is-sharing-genetic-data-with-drug-giant/.

Stuart Leavenworth, "DNA Testing Is Like the 'Wild West.' Should It Be More Tightly Regulated?" *Anchorage Daily News*, June 9, 2018. www.adn.com/nation-world/2018/06/09/dna-testing-is-like-the-wild-west-should-it-be-more-tightly-regulated/.

Stuart Leavenworth, "Who Is the Secretive Google Offshoot That Has Access to Ancestry's DNA Database," McClatchy DC Bureau, July 30, 2018. www.mcclatchydc.com/news/nation-world/article211324909.html.

John D. Loike, "Opinion: Consumer DNA Testing Is Crossing into Unethical Territory," *Scientist*, August 16, 2018. https://www.the-scientist.com/news-opinion/opinion--consumer-dna-testing-is-crossing-into-unethical-territories-64650.

Stephanie Pappas, "Could Genetic Testing Companies Violate Your Privacy?" Live Science, December 1, 2017. www.livescience.com/61079-why-dna-privacy-matters.html.

Ryan Suppe, "Your DNA Could Help Make New Drugs. But Should You Share It?" *USA Today*, August 30, 2018. www.usatoday.com/story/tech/talkingtech/2018/07/31/your-dna-could-help-make-new-drugs-but-should-you-share/853553002/.

Bruce Sussman, "DNA Testing Privacy Risks: DNA Company Starts Working with Pharmaceutical Giant," Secure World, July 30, 2018. www.secureworldexpo.com/industry-news/dna-testing-privacy-risks.

Sarah Zhang, "Big Pharma Would Like Your DNA," *Atlantic*, July 27, 2018. www.theatlantic.com/science/archive/2018/07/big-pharma-dna/566240/.

For Further Discussion

Chapter 1

1. Should statements on DNA testing company websites be taken as the last word on ownership? Why or why not?
2. If DNA test results could affect a person's relatives without their knowing, should test-takers inform their relatives that they're agreeing to DNA service agreements? Why or why not?
3. DNA testing companies claim that they will not share results without the consumer's agreement. Is it naïve or informed to believe them? What evidence can you provide on either side of the argument?

Chapter 2

1. According to Emily Mullin, DNA testing companies' real motive is to profit from consumers of at-home DNA test kits. How do you think this might motivate DNA data ownership?
2. Sarah Sunderman argues for US regulation of consumer DNA testing, borrowing from the German example. Is regulation needed? Why or why not? How would this affect DNA ownership rights?
3. Should DNA test results be protected as a civil right? How might ownership be protected if recognized as a civil right?

Chapter 3

1. According to Rebecca Robbins, law enforcement turns to DNA analysis to help solve crimes. Should investigators be given access? What criteria might govern this access?
2. Some have argued that DNA test results have the potential to harm family dynamics. How could safeguards protect families yet also help adoptees find birth parents?

3. Olivia Solon argues that anonymized genetic data is not possible. How might this impact DNA testing kit service agreements?

Chapter 4

1. Some experts have alleged that only testing companies profit when individual genetic information is sold to third parties, including big pharmaceuticals. Should consumers be compensated? If so, how?
2. Susan Young Rojahn maintains that anonymized genetic data can be traced to the individuals. What kinds of warnings should testing companies issue so users are aware of the risks?
3. Sheldon Krimsky and David Cay Johnston prepared a consumer's guide to genetic testing. Why is such a guide necessary?

Organizations to Contact

The editors have compiled the following list of organizations concerned with the issues debated in this book. The descriptions are derived from materials provided by the organizations. All have publications or information available for interested readers. The list was compiled on the date of publication of the present volume; the information provided here may change. Be aware that many organizations take several weeks or longer to respond to inquiries, so allow as much time as possible.

American Society of Human Genetics

6120 Executive Boulevard, Suite 500
Rockville, MD 20852
(301) 634-7300
website: www.ashg.org

The American Society of Human Genetics is a professional organization of some eight thousand human genetics specialists. Founded in 1948, it advances genetic research and promotes responsible genetic services. It seeks to understand human variation and promote public health.

Ancestry.com

1300 W. Traverse Parkway
Lehi, UT 84043
(801) 705-7000
website: www.ancestry.com

Ancestry started as a genealogy company and has now morphed into a digital-age genealogy service with DNA testing as one of its core services. It views itself as a science and technology company. The AncestryDNA database holds samples from more than ten million people worldwide.

Center for Genetics and Society

(510) 665-7760

website: www.geneticsandsociety.org

The Center for Genetics and Society was founded in Berkeley, California, in 2001. Among its goals are to encourage responsible use of genetic technologies and support equal access to medical applications. It is a nonprofit organization dedicated to social justice.

Center for Medicine in the Public Interest

757 Third Avenue, 20th Floor
New York, NY 10017
(212) 417-9169
email: info@cmpi.org
website: cmpi.org/

The Center for Medicine in the Public Interest is often called upon for expert statements about DNA test result privacy. It is a nonprofit research and educational organization focused on patient-centered health care. It also provides independent scientific analysis and commentary.

ConsumerAffairs.com

297 Kingsbury Grade, Suite 1025
Mailbox 4470
Lake Tahoe, NV 89449
(866) 773-0221
website: www.consumeraffairs.com

Consumer Affairs is a clearinghouse of hundreds of thousands of expert and verified reviews of consumer products. These include DNA testing kits from a variety of manufacturers.

Council for Responsible Genetics/International Center for Technology Assessment

5 Upland Road, Suite 3
Cambridge, MA 02140
phone: (202) 547-9359 x 24
email: GeneWatch@icta.org
website: www.councilforresponsiblegenetics.org/

The Council for Responsible Genetics was founded in 1983. It is a nonprofit, nongovernmental organization based in Cambridge, Massachusetts. Its goal is to distribute timely and accurate information concerning the ethical, social, and environmental implications of genetic technologies.

FamilyTreeDNA

(713) 868-1438
website: www.familytreeedna.com

FamilyTreeDNA was founded in 1989 by entrepreneur and lifelong genealogist Bennett Greenspan. It offers DNA testing kits and sophisticated analyses, including paternal and maternal results. It was the first company to offer DNA testing kits directly to consumers in 2000. It has two million users.

Federation of Genealogical Societies

PO Box 200940
Austin, TX 78720
(888) 347-1500
email: info@fgs.org
website: www.fgs.org

The Federation of Genealogical Societies, founded in 1975, serves the needs of genealogical societies in the United States and other countries. Its conferences and events discuss and explore the use of DNA testing.

International Society of Genetic Genealogy

email: https://isogg.org/contactus.html
website: www.isogg.org

Founded in 2005, the International Society of Genetic Genealogy was established specifically to advocate for the use of DNA testing in genealogical pursuits. The ISOGG is a noncommercial, nonprofit organization that educates others about the use of genetics in genealogy in workshops, forums, meetings, and through their wiki (https://isogg.org/wiki/Wiki_Welcome_Page).

MyHeritage

(800) 987-9000
website: www.myheritage.com

MyHeritage was founded in 2003 in Israel. It offers its members DNA testing services to learn more about their ancestors. A global company, it has more than ninety million users. Users of MyHeritageDNA can connect with relatives who also took the company's DNA test. The company's website offers information on DNA, family trees, access to research, and also presents interesting testimonials and case studies.

National Genealogical Society

6400 Arlington Boulevard, Suite 810
Falls Church, VA 22042
(703) 525-0050
email: ngs@ngsgenealogy.org
website: www.ngsgenealogy.org

The National Genealogical Society is a nonprofit organization founded in Washington, DC, in 1903. It is a leader in genealogical education. It has a division, GenTech, dedicated to bridging genealogy and technology. NGS offers conferences, publications, and educational courses for beginners and advanced family historians alike.

23andMe

899 W. Evelyn Avenue
Mountain View, CA 94041
(650) 938-6300
website: www.23andme.com

23andMe is an internet company in Silicon Valley with a mission to help people access, understand, and benefit from the human genome. It manufactures and distributes the 23andMe DNA testing kit. The company has more than five million genotyped customers worldwide. It was founded in 2006.

Bibliography of Books

Blaine T. Bettinger, *The Family Tree Guide to DNA Testing and Genetic Genealogy*. Cincinnati, OH: Family Tree Books, 2016.

Blaine T. Bettinger and Debbie Parker Wayne, *Genetic Genealogy in Practice*. Arlington, VA: National Genealogical Society, 2016.

Angie Bush, *Genetic Genealogy Basics*. Baltimore, MD: Genealogical Publishing Company, 2016.

Christopher Challender Child, *Using DNA in Genealogy*. Boston, MA: New England Historic Genealogical Society, 2014.

David R. Dowell, *NextGen Genealogy: The DNA Connection*. Santa Barbara, CA: Libraries Unlimited/ABC-Clio, 2015.

Kerry Farmer, *DNA for Genealogy*. St. Agnes, SA, Australia: Unlock the Past, 2017.

Lasse Folkersen and Pak Sham, *Understand Your DNA: A Guide*. Singapore and Hackensack, NJ: World Scientific Publishing Co., 2019.

Justin Healy, *Human Genetics and Ethics*. Thirroul, NSW, Australia: Spinney Press, 2018.

New York Times Editorial Staff, *DNA Testing: Genealogy and Forensics*. New York, NY: New York Times Educational Publishing, 2019.

Christine Scodari, *Alternate Roots: Ethnicity, Race, and Identity in Genealogy Media*. Jackson, MS: University Press of Mississippi, 2018.

Beth Skwarecki, *Genetics 101: From Chromosomes and the Double Helix to Cloning and DNA Tests, Everything You*

Need to Know about Genes. New York, NY: Adams Media, 2018.

Diahan Southard, *Breaking Down Brick Walls with DNA.* Rhome, TX: Genealogy Gems Publications, 2018.

Tamar Weinberg, *The Adoptee's Guide to DNA Testing: How to Use Genetic Genealogy to Discover Your Long-Lost Family.* Cincinnati, OH: Family Tree Books, 2018.

Paul Woodbury, *Developing a DNA Testing Plan.* St. Agnes, SA, Australia: Unlock the Past, 2018.

Ronnee K. Yashon and Michael R. Cummings, *Genetic Testing: What Do We Know?* New York, NY: Momentum Press, 2018.

Index